Wilt, Ike,

and Me

A Personal Memoir of an
American Dream
and Beyond

David Richman

Wilt, Ike & Me
A Personal Memoir of an American Dream & Beyond
By David Richman

A paperback and e-book copy of this book were published
in 2018 by Better Angels Publishing Co.

Better Angels Publishing Company, Philadelphia, PA.
www.betterangelspublishing.com

ISBN-10: 1975914252
ISBN-13: 978-1975914257
LCCN: 2017913637

For Sally & Emmy and Clare & Ike

To Prem Rawat, in
Deepest Appreciation

Contents

Acknowledgments

Over the years, I've become fond of a concept called Inter-Dependent Co-Arising. While it has a lot of different meanings, the simplest one is that we all contribute to each other's betterment.

As far as this book is concerned, I've certainly had a lot of help and encouragement with it. My hope is that everyone who has supported it will also benefit from their involvement, and that a positive circle of influence will continue to grow. There are a few people I would especially like to thank.

The idea for this project was originally hatched over some great lunches with my old friend Charlie Inlander, who has served as my mentor. My cousin, Jay Shor, who was like a son to my father, has stood behind me all the way, not just with this project, but from the very beginning. And my good friends, Elliot Schnier, Bill Goldstein and Sharon Segal, have gone far beyond the call when needed.

My whole family has been extremely encouraging, especially my brother Mike Richman and my sister Sybil Gabay, along with my siblings in law – Jude & Jontz Johnson, Robert Stein, and Nancy & Steve Swift.

I've also had a great group of friends and associates that have helped considerably. Jeff Shreiber, Gil Hanson,

Michael Goldstein, Alexandra Golaszewska, and Ross Cameron were instrumental in production. David Fineman, Julie Goldstein, Mary Kane, Andrew Kleeman, Ron Nissenbaum, Bruce Segal, Dan Sossaman, Vickie Spangler, Debbie Weiner and Jim Vuko have all been tremendously supportive, as well.

Then, there's my immediate family. Emma Clare, our daughter who was named after my father and mother, has been the light of our lives since day one, and has been an invaluable resource for me on every level, as always.

And my wife, Sally, who besides providing me with constant, and often extremely needed emotional and psychological support, also played a major role in the creative process. She was the primary editor, but more importantly, she was the project's sounding board. Ultimately, her feelings about every part of the piece were always my guidepost, and this book wouldn't be what it is without her.

Finally, in 1971, I was lucky enough to stumble upon a teacher of inner growth named Prem Rawat. It would take a much better writer than me to express the profound benefits I've gotten from his inspiration, but the word "Boundless" would be a good place to start.

So, my sincerest thanks to everyone, in hopes that we all continue to arise together.

— D.R.

Introduction

"Wilt, Ike, and Me," is a personal memoir with three main characters—Wilt Chamberlain, Ike Richman, and me, Ike's son David. It starts in 1965, when America was still in the early stages of the massive cultural revolution that would change it forever.

Wilt was one of the greatest athletes in history. He dominated the NBA for 14 seasons, and even though he retired decades ago, 72 of his records still stand. He passed away in 1999, but remains a major figure in the pantheon of American sports, and is an enduring popular icon as well.

Ike was a prominent Philadelphia attorney and a highly respected civic leader. A brilliant entrepreneur, among his other significant achievements, he founded the Philadelphia 76ers. Also, as Wilt's close friend, personal lawyer and primary financial advisor; he was essentially his second father.

And me, I was a typical American kid, a Baby Boomer who was lucky enough to grow up around some rather extraordinary people.

Although much of its action does revolve around basketball, this is not an ordinary sports book. That's only one part of a larger picture. As a true story, it has a lot of different layers to it, but that's the way real life is—more than just a one-dimensional journey. We all run far deeper than that.

It may be a little different from your expectations, so I thought a quick introduction might help. As it begins, my father makes the incredible trade that brings Wilt to the 76ers. Soon after, he moves him into our house for the rest of the season. A tenth grader, I was almost sixteen and, as you can imagine, it turned into a pretty wild ride for me.

Part Two is a flashback, showing how it all began. It weaves the path from my father's early career, through some of my formative experiences with him, to the time when Wilt enters our lives. My father eventually forms the 76'ers, and under his guidance, within two short years, the NBA title is clearly within our grasp.

But then, everything dramatically changes. Tragedy strikes, and my father dies of a massive heart attack. With my world turned upside down, I am plunged into a state of grief and loss.

However, there's another, unexpected side to the story. I had some rather mysterious experiences surrounding his death. You could call them "metaphysical," but "unexplainable" works just as well. Although much of it was inspiring, I was young and unprepared, and the whole thing was an enormous shock.

At first, I decided to leave this part out of the book. It didn't quite fit with the rest of the story and I thought people might be put off by it. But then I figured—this is a memoir, and these things actually did happen to me. And besides, like it or not, we all have to face death sooner or later. So, I left it in.

My life moved on and so did my adventures with Wilt and the team. We won the NBA Championship in 1967, and it was a tremendous triumph.

Ultimately, you can look at "Wilt, Ike, and Me" in

a lot of different ways. While it's definitely a sports story, it's a family saga as well. And set against the backdrop of America's radically changing cultural landscape, it's also a social chronicle. While it's filled with life's dramatic triumphs and tragedies, its real hero is the human heart, and its extraordinary capacity to transcend time and death.

Set in a more innocent era, it gives an inside look at some truly epic characters. Wilt was the quintessential great guy—smart, funny, and extremely charismatic. And besides his legendary athletic talents, his heart was even bigger than he was.

Ike had a noble character, with a brilliant instinct for people. Along with high moral standards, he had a great sense of humor. And it was all mixed-in with a practical genius for deal-making and basic "horse sense." As Wilt always said, he was one of a kind.

And me? While I'm not an epic character, I did take my generation's trip from the Mickey Mouse Club to the Grateful Dead, and beyond. And believe me, that was one magical mystery tour.

Hopefully, the book will keep you entertained, and maybe even offer a few things that might be useful down the road. Personally, I've had almost as much fun writing it, as I had living it.

So, let me tell you what happened.

Part 1

1

The Wizard Claps His Hands

I was in tenth grade. It was a Sunday night after dinner, and I was up in my room, in a mild panic. On Friday I had gotten a ton of homework for the weekend, but I had put it off, not even looking at it. Now my back was against the wall. It was "do or die" time, and there wasn't a lot of sand left in the hourglass. Unfortunately, this was nothing new. I had been doing the same thing every weekend for the whole semester.

I sat down to get started, but as always, as soon as I opened my textbook, I ran into a wall of guilt and fear. I felt guilty because once again, I had put the whole thing off until the last minute. I had warned myself a million times not to do this, but for the millionth time, I didn't listen. And I was afraid I was going to do a lousy job because I was out of time and really had to rush.

So, I did what I always did, I put the radio on. I kept the volume low, and soon, like aspirin for a headache, the familiar sound of rock 'n roll soothed away the guilt and fear. With my foot tapping to the rhythm, I finally got down to work.

After a little while, I thought I heard my father coming up the stairs. We lived in a split-level suburban home. My parents' room was on the first floor, and my older sister, Sybil, and I had the upstairs to ourselves. My big brother, Mike, was already long gone, married and in law school.

My father didn't make the trip upstairs all that often. And when he did, it was usually for something unusual. He walked into my room and sat down on the bed.

"Turn it off," he said, nodding toward the radio.

He was wearing his relaxed weekend clothes, which I always liked. As an attorney, most of the time, he was in a suit and tie. Now, he was casual, down to his Egyptian leather sandals, which he'd gotten on his last trip to Israel with my mother. They were replicas of the ones worn by ancient royalty and she said they made him look like the Pharaoh was one of his clients.

I got up, turned the radio off, and looked at him. In legal circles, he was well-known for his poker face, but I could usually tell his mood the second I saw him, and I knew immediately that something was up. He was leaving for the NBA All-Star Game in St. Louis in the morning, but it was clear he hadn't climbed the stairs just to say good-bye.

"So, listen," he said. "I decided to tell you something, but you have to understand that you are the only person I'm telling this to. Nobody else is going to know about it. This is just between me and you."

He paused and looked at me for a few seconds.

"To tell you the truth, I thought about not telling you this at all, because once I do, you can't say a word about it to anyone. And I'm not kidding. You can't tell a soul. Absolutely no one. This is top secret."

He was dead serious and just sat there, waiting for

me to acknowledge that I understood what he had said, and agreed to it. He didn't move.

"Sure," I said casually. "I won't tell anyone."

"OK, good." He paused and then with a somewhat subtle smile, said, "I just got Wilt!"

I didn't know what he meant. "Got Wilt to do what?" was my first thought, but I didn't say anything. He obviously was referring to his longtime client and close personal friend, Wilt Chamberlain. But Wilt had been out of our lives for quite some time. We had seen a lot of him when he played for the Philadelphia Warriors, but the team had been sold to San Francisco a few years earlier, and he lived out west now. I just looked at my father and waited for him to clarify himself.

"I got him," he said. "I got him in a trade. It's done. We just closed the deal on the phone. I just hung up." Now he broke into a big smile. "He'll be on the 76ers within a week. He's with us now."

"Oh my God!" I replied. I'd love to be able to say that I had a more profound comment, but I was dumbstruck. Not only was I excited by the incredible news; I was also deeply relieved. I knew that my father's long, dark days would finally be coming to an end and I almost burst into tears.

It had been a rough road since he and his partner had purchased the Syracuse Nationals in 1963, moved them to Philadelphia and turned them into the 76ers. The idea was risky from the start and almost nothing had gone right. It had been a costly move and they continued to lose a lot of money.

The fans never accepted the team. They were just a bunch of old rivals and attendance was dismal, with most games playing to empty houses. The press constantly criticized everything he did, and they were pretty mean.

Still, he never complained about it or doubted what he was doing. He said things weren't going to happen overnight and we were in it for the long haul. He always wore a brave face, but we were as close as a father and son could be, and I knew how bad it was. And for a kid, when one of your parents is going through a hard time, it casts a shadow over your whole world.

But now, suddenly everything was completely different. He had done the impossible and we both knew things were about to change dramatically.

He stood up and so did I. He held out his hand to me, and I shook it. He had a great handshake, with an innate sense of strength in it, somehow imparting a trust in the power of the good. Suddenly, he grabbed me and gave me a big hug. We embraced for a moment, then he turned and left.

As he walked down the stairs, he clapped his hands sharply, three times. It was an old habit he did when he was excited. He had one of the loudest hand claps you can imagine, and it would make your ears ring. As I heard it echo down the stairway, he sounded like a wizard who had conjured up a magic spell and was about to impress it into the world.

2

Eyes on the Skies

The next morning when I went to school, everything was normal except now, I was in on a secret that was about to blow the whole sports world apart. For the first few hours of the day, it was an amazing feeling to have such inside knowledge. Nobody knew what I knew, and it was incredible.

But to my surprise, it wore off pretty quickly and was replaced by an uncomfortable feeling of isolation. We human beings are social animals and we love to talk, especially when we have something exciting to say. My father had just pulled off the trade of the century and I couldn't breathe it to a soul. For the first time in my life, I felt cut off from my world and I really didn't like it.

On Tuesday, to ease the pressure, I came up with a short, crafty phrase: "Eyes on the skies, here comes the Dipper." I would say it to just a few close friends and they would look at me like I was either a little nuts or I knew something special. They had no idea what I was talking about, so I didn't violate my promise. But it still helped get some of the weight off my chest.

"The Dipper" is a shortened form of Wilt's favorite nickname, "The Big Dipper." From the time he was in junior high, he was so tall that he always had to dip his head down to walk under a doorway. He had to do it all day long, and his friends started calling him "The Big Dipper." They shortened it to "The Dipper" and eventually just to "Dip."

"Wilt the Stilt" was his most famous nickname, but the truth is, he really hated it. Some press guy had coined it, and he was stuck with it for the rest of his life. But it really rubbed him the wrong way. A stilt was rigid and stiff. But "The Big Dipper" was a name from the heavens. It had a glow, like it was written in the stars.

Wednesday night, the NBA All-Star Game was played, and Friday morning, my isolation from the rest of the world came to an end. My father broke the astounding news to the press—Wilt Chamberlain would be joining the 76ers.

The entire sports world exploded and in Philly, pure pandemonium broke out. Our beloved hero was coming back home, and nobody could believe my father had been able to pull off this miracle. The papers were full of praise for him and said it was a new beginning.

He flew back that afternoon and was home in time for Friday-night Shabbat dinner, which he never missed. He stood quietly at the head of the table and recited the prayers over the wine and the bread, the same way he always did, no matter what had happened during the week before, for good or for bad.

The next day, all hell broke loose—in a good way. And so, it began.

***

Things got off to a rocky start. As soon as the trade was announced, Wilt told the press that he planned to retire from basketball at the end of the season. He would play out the year in Philadelphia, and then he was done. He said he had told Ike clearly that he was going to quit, and he urged him not to waste his money on the trade. It wouldn't be worth it. His mind was made up. He was out.

Ike responded in typical Ike fashion. "I think I might be able to talk him into staying with us," he told the reporters. And that was all he had to say on the subject.

Even though Wilt had been upfront with him about his plans, my father and his partner decided to go forward with the trade anyway, and they laid out a ton of cash to close the deal. Wilt shrugged, wrapped up his affairs in San Francisco, and arrived in Philadelphia a few days later.

His first practice with the team was on January 20 and about six hundred fans showed up to watch. His first game was the next night, against his old team, the San Francisco Warriors. About seven thousand people came out, which far exceeded our largest crowd to date. The new 76ers won handily by nine points, and the fans were warming up. But the following three-game miniseries with the Boston Celtics really did the trick.

The first game was two days later, on a Saturday night, and it was sold out. The arch rivalry from previous years pitting Wilt against Bill Russell and the champion Celtics was suddenly on again, and the air was electric. It was a tight battle all the way. But in a thrilling climax, the 76ers, led by a great performance by Wilt, pulled it out—to the delight of the fans, as well as the press.

The next game was in Boston, and it was obviously payback time. The Celtics gave us a shellacking on national TV in front of their home crowd, and we lost by 17. Now the stage was set for the third game, the rubber match, which took place two nights later back in Philly on Friday night, January 29.

It was standing room only, and the excitement in the air was at a fevered pitch. You would have thought it was a championship game. From the time they came out on the court, Wilt and his new team delivered. They blew the Celtics out of the building, beating them soundly by 13. As the team left the court, the crowd was on its feet, stomping in wild appreciation. The press went crazy and the city fell in love.

So, within less than two weeks of the big trade, the 76ers, this dull team of former rivals that nobody cared about, suddenly were hometown heroes. It was a magical transformation, and my father, as the General Manager, sat confidently at the helm of his mighty new ship, thrust it into full throttle, and took it out into the open sea.

Needless to say, it was high times for me. Just turning sixteen and being in your first year of high school was exciting enough by itself. Now, things had gone to an almost surreal level.

3

My Room Becomes Olympus

About two weeks later, when I came home from school, I went up to my room as usual. But for some reason, my mother and our domestic helper (or maid, back then), Geneva, were in there, moving all the furniture around.

"Wilt's moving in," my mother said to me, nonchalantly, as I walked into the room. "Daddy's making him."

"Really?" I said, surprised. "When's he coming?"

"We don't know yet. But it's gonna be soon."

They moved an end table from one side of the room to the other, put it down, picked up their lit cigarettes from a nearby ashtray and each took a drag. They were both major smokers, along with everyone else in the house. My mother smoked Kents, with its Micronite filter. But Geneva's brand was Lucky Strike—straight up, no filter. Between the two of them, they exhaled gigantic plumes of gray smoke that looked like exhaust from a Rust Belt factory.

"We're moving you into the guest room," my mother said.

She was always in total control of everything that went on around the household, and Geneva was her stalwart companion. Their relationship went back to the week I was born, when Geneva was just seventeen. My grandmother knew her family from the old neighborhood in South Philly and had brought her over to meet my mother. Something clicked immediately between them, and my mother hired her on the spot.

They were the same height and weight, with almost identical body types. My mother gave her some clothes out of her closet, and that was it. Geneva stayed with our family until she died about sixty years later. I never knew life without her.

I've often been asked what it felt like when I first heard that Wilt was moving in. After all, I was about to have the most famous sports star in the world living in the room next to me.

The fact is, I don't think I gave it a second thought. My father said something had to happen, and so here it was, happening. That's pretty much the way things went around him.

Nobody ever told me, but it turned out that Wilt was having some trouble with his pancreas. My father wanted to keep him close, so he could watch over his diet, but he mainly wanted to limit his partying, especially his trips to New York.

My mother picked up a heavy end table by herself and carried it across the room. She was a petite woman, only about five-two, with pin-straight, dark-brown hair and a slight frame. But she was a force of nature unto herself and nothing ever stopped her. Whatever the word sinew means, she had it in spades.

The first time I saw it was when I was about four years old. We had gotten a new family dog, Chaser, which was the size of a small pony. He was a beautiful reddish-brown mixture of a Boxer and a German Shepherd.

He was bigger than I was, and we fell in love with each other on the spot. We were always together. Truly a gentle giant, at my nap time, I would lie down with him at the top of the stairs and gaze into his deep brown eyes and drift off to sleep, rubbing his velvety nose. Later, I would wake up with my head on his chest.

But his breed was a guard dog as well, and if he sensed any danger near us, he would turn into a raving maniac, ready to attack any intruder who approached. The mailman, milkman, and bread man all knew to walk softly when they came to our house.

One day, Chaser was lying in the hallway near the front door, which was wide open. The storm door was all that separated him from the outside world. I was playing at the top of the stairs, and my mother was in the kitchen.

Suddenly, for no apparent reason, he started growling angrily. Then, in an outburst of fury, he jumped right through the glass window of the storm door, exploding it to pieces. With shattered glass all over the front porch, he stood there barking in a mad rage, and wouldn't stop.

My mother came flying out of the kitchen, opened the door, and grabbed him by the collar. His front legs and paws were bleeding.

"Stop it, Chaser! Stop it!" she commanded, yanking him by the collar. With all his might, he tried to break free, but amazingly she was too strong for him and pulled him back. "Now stop it!" She jerked his collar sharply.

He settled his massive body down but kept snarling. Something dangerous was in the air and he was ready to fight it with everything he had. My mother looked around but didn't see anything unusual. That didn't matter to her. She had grown up on a farm and had a special connection with animals. She said they could see things that we couldn't, like they could peer into a different dimension or something.

"It's OK." She soothed him and patted his head. "It's OK. We're fine now, Big Fella. We're fine." She massaged his neck deeply. After a few minutes, he relaxed, and she led him back inside.

As I watched from my high perch, she laid him down on a big towel. While he kept panting, she carefully pulled shards of glass out of his legs and put mercurochrome on all his cuts. Whatever it was that had happened, they were clearly in it together.

"We're going to have to give Wilt half your closet," my mother said, snapping me back to the present. She took some of my clothes out and put them into a large open bag that Geneva was holding. Soon the right side of the closet was empty.

After that, we put my two twin beds together, side by side so Wilt could sleep diagonally across them. My mother gave me some rope and I got down on the floor and tied the frames together. She put a large fitted sheet on top, making an improvised king-size bed for him.

As big as it seemed, it still wasn't enough. There were a lot of mornings when I would sneak into the room to get something while he was still asleep. Even lying diagonally across the bed, his feet stuck out over the other side. Like everything else in this world, it was just too small for him.

Finally, after the bed was made, my mother laid out two oversized beach towels for him to use in the shower. The three of us stood in the doorway for a minute. My mother and Geneva lit new cigarettes, filling the room with fresh exhaust. We were ready for the big man.

***

Sure enough, a few days later, Wilt's friend and part-time driver, Archie, drove him over. They came at about four in the afternoon. The team had some time off, and then they were going into a home stretch. Wilt carried a bunch of suits from the dry cleaner over his shoulder, and Archie carried two big suitcases as they came up the stairs.

"Hey, Big Guy," Wilt said to me and walked straight into my room.

"Hey," Archie said, echoing him, as he walked by me.

Wilt had called me Big Guy, and I liked it. He used to call me Little Guy, but that was in the old days, back when I was nine and he played for the Warriors.

He put his clothes in the closet next to mine, which immediately produced a ridiculous sight. His suit jackets went almost down to the floor, and my stuff hanging next to them suddenly looked like they belonged to a first grader.

When you were around Wilt in a normal setting, like in your home, it was amazing how big he really was. You didn't get a true sense of it at a game. Even though the program said he was seven-one and weighed three hundred pounds, he was in an open arena playing next to a bunch of other giants. But in the normal world, it was completely different. I'd always thought our house was pretty big until he showed up. Suddenly it felt like a dollhouse.

He and Archie were both in goofy moods and were laughing a lot. I couldn't quite pick up on it, but they had been in the nightclub Wilt owned up in Harlem the night before. Supposedly, somebody had said something to an author named James Baldwin, who was a friend of Wilt's, and a glass of wine had gotten thrown. It had all worked out OK and turned into a big joke.

Wilt sat down on the bed. Archie picked up the phone and made a call. I heard him ask for somebody named Stella. Wilt turned, looked at me, and gave me a big smile. Unexpectedly, it hit like a lightning bolt. Even in a casual situation, he was packing a ton of charisma and the air around him always crackled.

Archie started talking to Stella on the phone, and I could hear that some plans were being made. Wilt got off the bed and walked me out of the room into the hall.

"Let's do something fun tomorrow," he said. He looked back at Archie, who was still in the middle of his conversation. He gave me another big smile and patted me on the top of my head. "Nice hair," he commented, and went back in the room and closed the door. They went out a little while later.

I went to sleep that night and never heard Wilt come in. The next morning, before I left for school, his door was closed. I wanted to see if he had come home, so I snuck over and cracked it open a slit. Sure enough, he was diagonally slung across the two beds, sound asleep. It was kind of hard to believe. There he was, this world-famous giant superstar in my room, looking like a golden-brown Greek god, peacefully sleeping-off a wild night on Mount Olympus.

4

Four-Deck War

Wilt had been out with Archie for most of the next day, and he came back after dinner. I heard him come in and start hanging around with my parents in the living room. I sat at my desk, stared into my history book, and tried to make sense out of something called the Dredd-Scott Decision, some Civil War issue.

I must have become really focused, because the next thing I knew, Wilt was standing in the room, reading the book over my shoulder. I looked up at him. "History can wait for another night," he said. "Come on in."

I got up and went into the room with him. He had brought over his own clock radio and flipped it on. It was set to the only jazz station in the city, which quickly pointed out one of the major differences between us. When it came to music, I was all rock and roll and he was pure jazz.

I couldn't stand that music. It had no hook, and there was nothing to sing along to. I was into bite-size songs with catchy melodies and a beat you could dance to. His stuff sounded like it came from another planet.

He knew a lot of jazz greats from his Harlem nightclub. They used to stop in and do late-night jam sessions that could go on until morning. He loved it and was a real aficionado. I found it unbelievably annoying, but I put up with it. After all, he was our houseguest, not to mention the fact that he was Wilt Chamberlain.

He went into the bathroom across the hall. He started washing his hands and asked me to get him another towel. When I handed it to him, I couldn't help feeling bad that everything was so small. He was stooped over because his head was taller than the ceiling, and the soap, the sink, and the towels were all miniatures to him. He looked like he was confined in a birdcage, which is the way it was most of the time for him, wherever he went.

We went back into the room. He was wearing jeans and a standard white oxford shirt. He took off his shoes and socks and stretched out on the floor. "Got any cards?" he asked.

I had a bunch of decks on a shelf, and he had me shuffle up four of them. We split them in half and got into a four-deck game of War, which was something that we did—not only for most of that night but for many more nights to come.

It was a perfect game for us. It required no skill or strategy at all. You didn't have to concentrate, and you could have a random conversation about anything. You just turned over cards and whoever had the higher card won the hand. That was it. There was nothing to do but relax, hang out, and have a good time. And the four-deck version hardly ever ended. It just went on and on.

That was probably the first time we ever hung out on the floor together, which was a great equalizer. Now, he was just really long rather than really tall. We were eyeball-to-eyeball with each other and could relax and talk normally. When he was standing up, talking to him was like shouting to someone up a mountain.

As we kept playing, we got into a ton of subjects, mostly about me and my life. He asked me all about school, what my favorite subjects were, how I was doing getting ready for my driving test, and of course about girls. How was it going? Was I playing the field or going out with anyone specific?

It didn't occur to me at the time, but he knew all about the stage of development I was heading into. The biological impulses of a boy turning sixteen were certainly no mystery to him. He was twenty-nine and one of the most eligible and experienced bachelors on the planet.

It started to get late for me, and I had to get back and finish my homework. I never knew what he did after I went to sleep. He used to have me take the phone out of the room when I left so it wouldn't bother him in the morning. I did, said good-night and tried to get back into my homework. But I had no more concentration left for the Civil War.

5

You Know What, Ike?

The team went on the road for a few days, and I didn't see Wilt again until the following Saturday night at the New York Knicks game on our home court. But the Wilt I saw at a game was completely different from the casual guy I was rooming with at home.

Now he was the legend, the superstar, the absolute center of attention, and the fans loved him. But it also came at a cost. They had all come specifically to watch him play and he was constantly scrutinized and critiqued by the press and on TV, so the pressure on him was intense. And on top of that, although he was the crowd's beloved hero, he was also the opposing team's primary target. They would do everything they possibly could, clean or dirty, to try to stop him.

In a lot of ways, basketball is like an improvised, graceful ballet. But under the basket, it's pure combat, and Wilt always had a major fight on his hands at every game. His opponents would double or triple-team him. They would lean on him, push him, shove him, and hold him. But they could never stop him. The fans couldn't get enough and to my father's relief, the attendance figures finally started to climb into the respectable neighborhood.

That Saturday night, my father, mother, and I drove down to the Knicks game together. As usual, we got there about an hour early. My father disappeared into the team's locker room, and my mother and I went out to our seats. In a little while, we were joined by my brother and his wife. Soon after, my sister and her boyfriend arrived.

In those days, the games were held in a large municipal auditorium called Convention Hall, which had opened in 1931. It was a giant performance venue with the main stage at one end. Every major act that came to Philly played there, including the Beatles, the Rolling Stones, and Frank Sinatra.

However, when the center part of the seating was removed and replaced with a basketball court, it became a perfect arena for a game. It could still seat more than 9,600, but it was a really tight fit. The fans were practically on top of the court, and it was incredibly loud in there. The hall had a curved ceiling that was acoustically designed for music performances. But during a game, it became a powerful amplifier, magnifying the crowd noise to earsplitting proportions.

And on top of all that, the air in the place was horrible. It would fill up with cigarette smoke before the game even began. About half the crowd was chain-smoking, including a lot of the players, who routinely caught a couple of drags during every time-out. My father usually had a huge lit cigar going most of the time.

As usual, the place was empty when we first got there and gradually started to fill up. About twenty minutes before game time, my father walked out of the back area with two of his oldest friends, Eddie Gottlieb and Dave Zinkoff, known to the world as Gotty and Zink. They were both longtime Philadelphia legends.

My father sat down at the scorer's table, right next

to the 76ers bench, and Gotty sat down next to him. Zink went to the center of the table and sat down behind a large silver microphone.

Gotty was fifteen years older than my father. They had met when he was my father's gym teacher at South Philadelphia High School. One of the original founders of the NBA and the owner of the first Philadelphia team, the Warriors, Gotty was still the single most important person in professional basketball at the time. My father was his personal attorney and had been the team's General Counsel as well.

Dave Zinkoff, generally called "The Great Zink," was the most famous public-address announcer in the country. His voice was a Philadelphia institution. Although his style has been copied all over the world, he was the acknowledged original of the art form. And he had an intuitive genius for orchestrating the crowd's energy. With his flamboyant style, he could whip them into a frenzy with a drawn-out word, a catchy phrase, or even just a pause.

At one point, my mother pulled out her knitting needles from the canvas bag she carried and started methodically knitting away. It was something she did at every game for as long as I could remember.

I looked over at my father to see if he had noticed. He and Gotty were in the middle of one of their endless sidebar conversations, and he didn't seem to care at all. I wasn't surprised by his non-reaction, given the conversation that had gone on between my parents during the car ride in.

As he had turned onto the expressway, my father had told my mother that he had finally gotten the public relations report he had been waiting for. He had hired a PR firm to come up with suggestions on how to make the games more exciting. At the end of the report, it mentioned a certain woman who sat in the front row at every game, knitting.

The firm felt the sight of someone knitting at courtside was counterproductive, giving off an image of boredom. They said the woman should be told to stop immediately.

"That's an interesting point," my mother said, pulling out a cigarette. "I never looked at it that way." She lit up.

"Me either," my father agreed.

"You know what, Ike?" She asked and took a deep drag. "Tell 'em to go to hell," she said, exhaling a huge amount of smoke which punctuated her words. She looked like a relaxed, fire-breathing dragon, completely at ease, knowing she had no real fight on her hands.

He responded in Yiddish and she snapped back at him in kind. They immediately launched into one of their private conversations, in a language they knew I didn't understand.

Yiddish was my father's native tongue, and they were both fluent in it. But they never taught it to their kids. They kept it to themselves. As soon as a conversation went into a subject they didn't want us to hear, they just dropped their Yiddish curtain around themselves and went off into their own world. They could do it at the drop of a hat.

Looking back on it, I think their ability to communicate openly in front of us, knowing we couldn't understand them, played an important role in shaping my inner makeup. Because of it, I never once heard them say anything unkind or derogatory to each other. Even though it probably had its downsides, in the long run I'm sure it kept a lot of crap out of my mind.

I could always tell how their Yiddish conversations were going just by their tone, and I knew this knitting thing was going nowhere. My mother clearly wasn't going to budge, and my father didn't care. He had hired the PR firm long before he got Wilt. We had the big guy now, and attendance was no longer an issue, so their opinion didn't really matter. One more Yiddish-only topic was going by the wayside.

***

It wasn't a sell-out crowd that night, but we still had more than eight thousand people in the hall, which was a big improvement. There were the usual pregame murmurings as the fans filtered in, bought candy and popcorn, and took their seats.

The Knicks trotted out and started doing their lay-up drills, and the crowd gave them a light chorus of polite Philadelphia booing, keeping it low-key. Then, the 76ers came out to an enthusiastic welcome. After the warm-up period ended, both teams went back to their benches and sat down.

Zink's voice boomed over the PA system. "Good evening, ladies and gentlemen, and welcome!" He went through a few pleasantries and then introduced the starting five of the Knicks. The fans tepidly booed as each player trotted onto the court.

Then, he started with the 76ers. As each player came out, the crowd got louder and louder. Soon, it was time for him to introduce Wilt, which he always saved for last.

"And now, at center..." The entire crowd rose to its feet and started cheering thunderously. "From Kansas University, and originally from Oooooooooverbrook High School..."

That did it. The long, drawn-out o in Overbrook drove them over the edge. You couldn't hear the rest of his announcement, but it was usually: "At seven-feet, one-inch, wearing number thirteen, Philadelphia's own, Wilt Chamberlain!" Everything was drowned out by a long, standing ovation.

Wilt came jogging out and joined the rest of the team. He looked around at the crowd and gave them one of his cool, confident, but somewhat coy smiles. He seemed relaxed, but he also had that steely-eyed gaze of the warrior, who knew what was coming and was ready for it.

The Knicks had a rookie named Willis Reed who went on to become a Hall of Famer. He was one of a new group of strong centers whose main goal was to challenge Wilt's dominance of the league. And that night, he did just that.

From the opening whistle, it was a tough, hard-fought game. The Knicks had come to play, and Reed gave Wilt a hard time at both ends of the court.

We always sat in the front row, courtside, under the basket -near the 76ers' bench. Our seats were only about two feet from the inbound line, so we were right in the middle of the action.

From that perspective, it was always a brutal scene. You could see every hit and hear every groan as the players constantly clobbered each other. They played Wilt dirty and I always took it personally. He was like a member of the family, and I couldn't stand what they did to him.

The game went back and forth, point by point, and the crowd was intimately involved in every play. At the end of the first quarter, we were ahead by six, 30–24. But the Knicks clawed their way back and outscored us by ten in the second. We were losing by four, 58–54 when the halftime buzzer blared.

Everybody in Convention Hall was relieved to be able to take a break as the players went back to the locker rooms and the fans lined up at the refreshment stands. For a few moments, the only sound you heard was the constant clicking of cigarette lighters.

6

Is It a Kosher Hot Dog?

Back then, a pro-basketball game was completely different from the non-stop entertainment spectacular it's become. In those days, it was just the game itself, along with the announcer. That was it. No music, no organ, no cheerleaders, and no extra entertainment. It was just you, the players and the game. And when halftime came, the place went dead quiet and you had a welcomed fifteen minutes to take it easy. You needed it.

My father always went back to the locker room with the team, and I went out into the lobby and got a snack, the same thing every time: a hot dog with mustard and relish, and a large Coke.

I did my usual routine, but as I was returning, I could see that Gotty was sitting in my seat, talking to my mother. So, I hung back for a while and ate my dog at the rear of the stands.

Gotty was the closest thing to an actual godfather I had in my life. He had never married, and we were kind of an adopted family to him. He was over all the time. He and Zink usually joined us for Passover and other similar occasions.

He knew my parents years before they were married, and had a particular fondness for my mother. He once gave her an engraved trophy, honoring her as a world-class "balabusta." As with a lot of Yiddish terms, it carries a few levels of meaning. While a balabusta is a fantastic homemaker and the queen of the household, she is also its spiritual guide, imparting sustenance and strength to her family.

Gotty could always break her up, and they were having a good laugh as he was talking to her. As I watched them, his face reminded me of my earliest memory of him, which also involved a hot dog and a lot of laughter.

I was probably about five. It was a Saturday afternoon, and my father and Gotty were sitting on the side porch of our first house. We lived in the middle of a three-square-mile section of Northeast Philadelphia called Oxford Circle, surrounded by thousands of other row homes that went on forever.

The building across the street from us was different from all the rest, however, and our side porch looked right at it. Instead of a series of row homes, it was just one, block-long building. The whole thing was dark brown, and everyone called it "the church."

Over time, I came to understand that it had something to do with something that had nothing to do with us. We were part of this one thing, this Jewish thing. And this church place was part of something else. That's about all I knew, except that in some vague way, it had something to do with God.

I didn't know much about God, other than he was this big, important guy who ran everything. I think he lived over at this place we went to a lot, called "the shul" (Yiddish for synagogue). I don't know if the God who lived at "the church" was the same guy as the one who lived at "the shul." It didn't seem possible because this place was so different, but he seemed to be going by the same name.

Anyway, on this particular Saturday, the church was having a big fair. Geneva took me over and they had all kinds of food there. My mother had given her some money to get me something to eat. They had some nice-looking hot dogs, so I picked one out. I started eating it, and Geneva took my hand and walked me back across the street. My father and Gotty were chatting away when my father saw me.

"What are you eating, Duvy?" he shouted over to me.

"A hot dog," I shouted back.

"Really?" He smiled but seemed to get a bit serious. "Is it a kosher hot dog?" I didn't answer right away, but I stopped eating it.

"Uh oh," I thought. Even though I was still very young, I was old enough to know that we followed these strict Jewish laws of eating called "kosher." It was a big deal, with all kinds of rules. You didn't eat meat with milk. Certain kinds of food were OK, but you never ate other stuff.

Suddenly, I had a bad feeling about the whole thing. Was this God over there, kosher? I don't know why, but I figured he probably wasn't. I had already taken a few bites of the hot dog and was chewing it as my father was talking to me, so I was in pretty deep. As far as answering his question about whether or not it was kosher, I decided to wing it.

"Sure!" I shouted back.

To my surprise, my stomach turned over and I felt an intense pang of guilt. I could hardly move, and my young mind started racing with fear.

I felt bad I had forgotten about the whole kosher thing in the first place. I had started eating it without thinking. It had never even occurred to me. So that was my first mistake. But now, to make it worse, I had lied to my father. Maybe it wasn't a real lie; maybe it was just that fib thing. Either way, I knew better. What if this God guy decided to strike me dead? I heard he did that sometimes.

"So, you really think that's a kosher hot dog?" my father said, puffing on his cigar. Then he looked me in the eyes and asked, "Where did you get it, David?"

I figured my best move was to tell the truth and let the chips fall where they may. "The church," I answered, and braced myself for the possible end of the world.

My father and Gotty suddenly burst out laughing like it was the funniest thing they had ever heard. My father looked like he was going to swallow his cigar. After a minute, he caught his breath.

"Oh, good," he said, still laughing. I looked at Gotty. The white parchment skin of his pale face was crinkled up in pure delight. "As long as it came from the church, then I'm sure you'll be fine," my father declared. "Don't worry about it," he added reassuringly. "You're OK."

I was relieved, but a little confused. Somehow "the church" and "kosher" didn't quite go together in my mind. Suddenly there seemed to be something man made about all this God stuff, but I didn't care. My father was happy, the sun was shining, and the dense shroud of guilt that had smothered me, evaporated into the warm light of day. I finished the hot dog and didn't give it another thought...

Meanwhile, back at the Knicks game, I was finishing my halftime hot dog. The teams came out and started shooting around. I saw Gotty stand up, so I walked back over to my seat.

"Where's your date?" he asked me as soon as he saw me.

"What?" I asked.

"You're old enough to bring a date to a game now, Big Boy." He looked around the hall. "You know, when we first started this thing, we started it as a combination dance and game. Remember that, Clare?"

"Of course, are you kidding?" my mother answered.

"Yeah, there would be a small dance first. Then, we'd play the game and finish it off with a really big dance—thirty-piece band and everything. It was incredible."

He started walking away but turned back to me and comically straightened his bow tie. "You're old enough now, kid."

***

The second half started. In no time flat, we were back into the heat of the action, and it was more intense than ever. The teams fought each other point for point. When the third quarter ended, we were up by two, 80–78. But, at the beginning of the fourth quarter, the magic happened. We were on defense, and Wilt was at the end of the court, under the basket. One of the Knicks took a shot and with perfect timing, he flew up high into the air, with his right arm fully extended. He not only blocked the shot but grabbed the ball in midair with his right hand.

It was such a rare sight that the crowd gasped. But that wasn't all. Our point guard, Hal Greer, had started running down the court to our basket as soon as Wilt grabbed the ball. I don't know how he did it because Greer was out of his sight line, but he threw a perfect ninety-four-foot bullet pass the entire length of the court, straight into Greer's hands, timed perfectly with his sprinting stride. Hal dropped in an easy lay-up, and the crowd went out of their minds.

It proved to be the proverbial game changer, and the momentum shifted. Wilt took it all to another level and dominated the game. He blocked more shots, grabbed tons of rebounds, and scored 19 of his 40 points.

The game turned into a rollicking rout, and we won by 19, 111–92. An elated and satisfied crowd started filing out of the hall.

***

We always hung around until the end of the night. I won't say that my father turned off the lights, but there would only be a few maintenance men left when we were ready to go. Somebody from the box office would usually give him some figures on the night's attendance. He'd sign something, and then we'd be finished.

That's about where we were when Wilt came out from the back area with Archie. They were driving down to Baltimore, where there was a game the next night. Wilt and my father went off and sat in the stands and talked together for a few minutes. Then, they both came over to where I was sitting with my mother.

Wilt told her he'd be back at the house in a day or two. He bent down and kissed her on the cheek, which he always did.

"So long, Clare," he said. "And thanks again for everything."

"Oh, come on," she said, smiling. "You know the place is yours." He smiled and gave me a quick wink. Then, he turned and walked over to Archie, and they left.

My father sat down next to my mother. They needed to discuss something. "This will only take a minute," he said to me. They spoke in English, so it wasn't private or anything.

I got up and walked over to the 76ers' bench, sat down and looked around the deserted auditorium, dimly lit by just the house lights. Two maintenance men were in the upper stands breaking down some wooden chairs and another crew was sweeping trash.

The constant clacking of the collapsing folding chairs, mixed with the rhythmic swishing of the brooms on the floor, produced a hypnotic sound. The emptiness of the cavernous hall, along with its superb acoustics, doubled the volume, as haunting echoes bounced off the walls. The reverberations seemed to come from everywhere and nowhere at the same time.

It was trance-like, and I sat there, staring off into space, sort of exhausted. The place was so empty, it was hard to believe it had just been filled to the rafters with thousands of screaming fans. Now, it was deserted, like nothing had ever happened.

It reminded me of being on the beach with my brother, building sand castles near the ocean. We would erect elaborate structures, complete with towers and tunnels, and work until it was almost dark. Then the next day when we'd come back, to our amazement, it would all be gone without a trace, completely washed away by the tide. We couldn't even figure out where our sand castles had been.

Like ocean waves breaking at the shore, the soft, rhythmic clean-up sounds continued, as I sat at courtside. I stared at the 76ers logo on the shiny floor in front of me. My father had designed it, with its circle of thirteen stars over the number seven. We all loved it. The gigantic auditorium was now completely still. And the vast stillness seemed to have a presence all its own.

"Come on, Shortstop," I heard my father call to me. I looked over and saw that my parents were walking toward the exit.

"OK, here I come," I replied. I got up and followed them, as arm in arm, they disappeared into the tunnel.

7

Titanic Walks

A couple of days later, the team came back to town. Wilt showed up at our house again, but this time for an extended stay. We fell into a regular daily routine. He'd generally be sleeping when I left for school in the morning. When I got home, he'd be either up in his room or out walking around the neighborhood. He took a lot of walks.

We lived in a community called Elkins Park, which is in Cheltenham Township, just north of Philadelphia. It's an upper-middle-class American suburb and has a lot of stretches where you can take some great long walks.

Our house was just a few hundred yards away from a large religious institution called Faith Theological Seminary, which was a training facility for future clergymen. But it didn't start out that way. When it was first built at the turn of the century, it was called Lynnewood Hall and was a 110-room Georgian-style palace from the Gilded Age. Finished in 1900, it quickly became known as the American Versailles and was considered the most magnificent estate outside of France.

It had luxurious gardens complete with huge fountains and ponds, and the home was filled with over two thousand artistic masterpieces. It was the center of a vast social network of the wealthiest and most powerful people in the land. There were legendary parties that went on all night, routinely ending with sumptuous sunrise breakfasts.

The mansion itself stands in the middle of a thirty-five-acre circle of land, enclosed by a black wrought iron fence. It was about a two-mile stretch from our house, around the estate, and back. Wilt would usually make the trip every day, sometimes going around twice.

Now, this was 1965 and in our neck of the woods, black people and white people generally didn't live in the same neighborhood. Things were basically segregated. Cheltenham has changed a lot over the years and is now a model of multicultural living. But back then it was completely different, and in our area, all the residents were white.

Soon the local grapevine was buzzing with news that a huge black man was regularly seen walking around the neighborhood near the seminary. A short time later, it became common knowledge that this mysterious giant was, in fact, Wilt Chamberlain and that he was living in Ike Richman's house.

Before you knew it, nearly everyone claimed they had seen him out on one of his famous walks and had gotten a wink, a wave, or a nod. One day, a school bus slowed down to a crawl, so all the kids could come over to one side and wave at him through the windows.

For most people, seeing Wilt up close was an experience they would never forget. Not only was he much bigger than they'd thought, he was also strikingly handsome and extremely charismatic, with an engaging personality and a great sense of humor. And he always had a slightly comical expression on his face, like he was in on some kind of inside, private joke. In essence, he was just unbelievably cool.

Memories of him never seem to fade. Although he walked that neighborhood over fifty years ago, people still tell me stories about seeing him. And they're all still smiling.

Lynnewood Hall always held something special for Wilt. He was fascinated with its architecture and loved to take it in from all the different angles he would see as he walked around its perimeter. As a world traveler, he had developed quite a discerning eye for art, architecture, and design. And this palace was a real masterpiece.

It was built by Peter Widener, who was a true embodiment of the American dream. Born in 1834 and starting out as a butcher, he made his first real money selling beef to the Union army during the Civil War. Then, he parlayed his holdings into a huge transportation company that he formed with his partner, William Elkins, the namesake of Elkins Park. He also helped start US Steel and American Tobacco, and ultimately became one of the wealthiest men in American history.

Unfortunately, his interests extended into the steamship business as well, and he owned a piece of the White Star Line. The RMS Titanic was one of his investments. He sent the elder of his two sons, George, over to England to celebrate the maiden voyage of the "unsinkable vessel." George, his wife, and their son occupied one of the premier luxury suites in first class.

The night of the iceberg tragedy, the Wideners were hosting a formal dinner party for the ship's captain, who was summoned from it when the collision occurred. Mrs. Widener survived the horrible ordeal, but both father and son went down with the ship.

Peter Widener was devastated. He withdrew from the world, retreated into Lynnewood Hall, and never really re-emerged from it. Within a few years, continuing to mourn the loss of his son and grandson, the old man died of a broken heart.

But the grand old mansion still remains. Its religious conversion didn't take place until 1952 and it was a monastery for about twenty-five years until the brotherhood finally closed-up shop. It's been abandoned for decades.

Now, after an age of neglect, with its insides gutted and its once-white limestone faded to a dull brown, it still holds its magnificent place in the sun, perhaps waiting for some dreamer to come along, with inspired visions of restoration and redemption.

Wilt knew all about Widener's Titanic connection and the place always got to him. I don't know if it was just plain spooky, or if it spoke to him on some profound level, maybe about our ultimate mortality. Whatever it was, I could always tell when he'd been there from his distant gaze as he walked back onto our street.

I didn't pay too much attention to it though. I'd usually be wrapped up with the primary occupation of my life at that time, which was getting ready for my driver's test. We had a long driveway next to our house, and I'd spend hours every day driving up and back, in forward and reverse, and making U-turns.

In reality, getting my license was a far bigger deal to me than having Wilt living at the house. That was great, but it was only going to be for a short period of time. Getting my driver's license was going to change my life completely. And that was going to be forever. I couldn't wait.

One day, after I got my learner's permit, Wilt decided that he should become my driving teacher. He told me that he was the best driver he knew and that he could teach me a lot. Of course, I immediately accepted the offer, although it seemed more like an order than an offer.

One of the main things about Wilt —and everyone who ever knew him would agree with this —no matter what the activity was, he thought he was the best at it. Or he could be if he applied himself. It wasn't that much of an ego thing; he just had a strong sense of self-worth and knew his capabilities.

He was even a great drinker, with a renowned ability to hold his liquor. Apparently, he could consume mass quantities of alcohol without ever getting drunk.

According to legend, one night in Moscow, when he was playing with the Harlem Globetrotters, Nikita Khrushchev got together with the team after a game and brought in a case of their best vodka. The drinks started flowing heavily and as the evening wore on, one by one, everyone had to call it quits. By the end of the night, it was just Wilt and Khrushchev sitting at the table together with an interpreter, slamming shots, trading jokes, and laughing their heads off.

As far as driving was concerned, Wilt did have some strong credentials. Besides routinely driving a sports car on a racetrack at 180 miles an hour, at the end of every season, he would drive from New York to Los Angeles, by himself, in one unbroken three-day trip, never stopping to sleep. He was an insomniac anyway, so it didn't bother him. He relished the time alone, away from the rest of the world, in a rare and welcomed state of solitude.

Anyway, we started cruising around together in my father's Cadillac. Wilt would sit in the back seat, taking up the entire space. But he would also lean the upper half of his body over the seat and take up the whole front passenger area as well. It felt like he was right next to me, or more like - all over me.

"Keep as much of your attention in the rearview mirror as you keep on the road," he would tell me, repeatedly. "Always watch your back."

Whenever I was about to make a turn, I'd hear, "Look out both sides before you turn. Both sides, always." As soon as I made the turn, it was, "Now look back into the rearview again. Look in the mirror. You always gotta watch your back."

It was nonstop and, as you can imagine, more than a little intimidating. I had spent months practicing in the driveway but had only driven on the street a few days. I was trying my best to concentrate but at every turn, I had this overwhelming giant barking directions into my ear. I had to get used to it, though. What else was I going to do?

Back home, I'd pull into the driveway and he would give me a blow-by-blow rundown on everything I had done right and then especially on everything I had done wrong. He even knew the names of most of the streets. Then, he'd wrap it all up with a final lecture/pep talk.

"Now, now listen," he would say with his slight stammer. "You, you, you always gotta watch out for the other guy, you dig? Nine times out of ten, it's the other guy who's gonna hurt you. You're gonna be cruisin' along just fine, and then some clown who's not payin' attention is gonna cross into the intersection and then—bam!" He'd smack his hands together, producing a sharp thunderclap right next to my head. With my ear still ringing, I'd hear him add, "See what I'm sayin'?" He used that phrase a lot. Then he'd smile at me. "But you're doing all right. We'll just keep at it. You're going to be fine."

8

A Change Is Gonna Come

Sometimes after Wilt and I finished driving, we'd shoot some baskets. He would stand under the hoop and rebound for me. I was a decent player. Nothing special, but I could hold my own in most of my neighborhood's backyard games.

Every so often, as he stood under the basket, he'd reach up flat-footed, grab the net, and straighten it out, which always amazed me. The only way I could ever touch the bottom of that net was on a ladder. At five-seven, I was on the short side and it was way out of my reach.

Even so, in those days, I was dreaming of playing point guard in the NBA and was sure I would grow up to be at least six-two. "Just you wait. One summer, you're gonna shoot up like a beanpole," people would tell me. Or at least that's what I thought I heard. But my mother was just over five feet, and my father was only five-eight, so I knew the odds were against me.

Still, shooting around by myself at home, I was an All- American. In my mind's eye, I was a great ball-player with a scholarship to Harvard. I'd have visions of myself showing-up at a string of galas with gorgeous débutantes on my arm. I was at least six-four, and I'm pretty sure I had blond hair and blue eyes as well.

But back in the real world, I had a much bigger problem than the future performance of my growth hormones. I was having a lot of trouble with parallel parking. No matter how hard I tried, I just couldn't get the hang of it.

So, one day Wilt decided that we should drive over the city limit to a commercial part of North Broad Street, where he could give me some pointers on how to squeeze into a parking space. He said it wasn't all that hard.

"I think you're good enough to listen to the radio now," he commented as we drove along. I turned it on, and soon, the deejay said it was time for the daily double, which was two songs in a row by the same artist. Then Sam Cooke came on singing "Another Saturday Night."

"Oh my God! My theme song," Wilt exclaimed. "Turn it up! Turn it up!"

I made it louder, but it wasn't loud enough for him. "Come on!" he said. I blasted it, and he started singing as we drove along. Along with his love of music, he had a fine singing voice and had even made a record once. He kept snapping his fingers along with the music, right next to my ear. His hand was probably three times the normal size, and every snap was like a firecracker exploding in my skull.

I did my best to concentrate, but this was crazy. I wasn't even a novice, and he was totally distracting. I started getting perturbed, but that was just one part of me. Another part felt like it was the coolest thing in the world.

Wilt had a happy smile when the song ended. But then the slow, haunting introduction of "A Change is Gonna Come" came on, and everything changed.

It was the final song of Sam Cooke's young life and the mood got somber as Cooke began to sing: "I was born by the river, in a little tent. And just like the river, I've been running ever since. It's been a long, long time coming, but I know, a change is gonna come. Oh yes, it will."

"I knew him," Wilt said over the music. "He came up to Paradise right before he died and sang a couple of numbers." The nightclub he owned was called Big Wilt's Smalls Paradise, but whenever he talked to me about it, he just called it "Paradise."

"They released this right after he got killed," he said.

We fell silent and listened to the rest of the song. When the last verse started, Wilt closed his eyes and sang along, his soul coming out of his mouth.

"It's been too hard living, but I'm afraid to die. 'Cause I don't know what's up there, beyond the sky. It's been a long, long time coming, but I know, a change is gonna come...Oh yes, it will."

When the song ended, I looked at him in the rearview mirror. His eyes were closed, and he was clearly in another world. But when he opened them, he spotted a parking space in front of one of the stores, which immediately brought him back from wherever he was and put him squarely on North Broad Street.

"OK, OK, this is perfect. Pull over," he said. We were near the busy shopping area of Broad Street and Olney Avenue. "OK. Come on, let's see what you can do."

I pulled up parallel to the car that was in front of the open space and tried to back in. But I started having all my usual troubles, cutting the wheel at the wrong time, either too early or too late. I had to keep pulling out and starting over, which I did four or five times, as he kept coaching me along.

"All right," he finally said. "It's not that hard. Here, let me help you. Just do what I tell you."

He jumped out of the car and stood on the sidewalk. "Turn the wheel," he shouted, gesturing with his hands. "Turn, turn. You gotta cut it harder."

I was focused on trying to park and pretty much lost touch with everything other than trying to squeeze the car into the space, which was probably too tight, to begin with.

"Wilt! Wilt! Hey, Wilt!" I heard someone shout. I looked over at the sidewalk where he was standing and there must have been forty kids surrounding him. I didn't know where they had come from. I was so wrapped up in what I was doing I hadn't seen them approach.

They were gathered around him like iron filings stuck on a magnet. I could see their faces, and they were all filled with joy, like they were unexpectedly getting a gift from on high. Quite simply, they were out of their minds.

Wilt looked at all of them for a minute and flashed them one of his ear-to-ear smiles, his enormous white teeth reflecting the sunlight back at them.

"Wilt! Sign this!" One of the kids held up a notebook with a pen.

"Yeah!" The other kids shouted and started scrambling for pens and papers. "Can we have your autograph? Please?"

He took a quick look at the small crowd and could see that more kids were starting to come. The buzz on the sidewalk was clearly underway.

"I can't, kids. I can't right now. I'm late for an appointment, and I really gotta go!" He touched his wrist, pointing to an imaginary watch.

Everybody groaned. "Oh no! Oh, come on, Wilt. Please? Come on!"

One kid had a basketball. He tossed it over to Wilt, who grabbed it in midair with his right hand. Then he stood tall and held the ball up high against the sky. He looked like the Statue of Liberty, with the ball at least nine feet in the air. The awestruck kids fell silent for a few seconds, gazing up at the living colossus who stood before them. Then he casually flipped the ball back to the kid, who caught it and seemed ready to leave his body in bliss.

"I'm sorry, kids. I really have to go." Wilt opened the back door of the car. "Be good, now!" he said and hopped in.

"Come on," he muttered to me, quietly but sharply. "Come on. We gotta get outta here right now!"

The scene on the street had turned into mini-mayhem. While we were there, about fifty other people, including a bunch of adults, had come rushing over. More were on their way. Wilt wanted me to move before any of them started surrounding the car, which would have blocked our exit and put us in a completely different situation.

I had been halfway into the space. As I pulled out carefully, he rolled the window down and leaned his head and shoulders out of the car. He waved to them with a hand that would be the biggest one they would ever see in their lives. And it was sure to grow in their memories as the years went by. "Be good, now," he shouted back to them as I pulled away. "Be good!"

This kind of thing had been going on with Wilt for years, and he had a specific way of handling it. Whenever a group gathered, he would quickly decide whether to sign autographs or not. And he would never start if he couldn't sign them all.

That would create a bad situation for the kids who missed out. And not only would they be disappointed, but it would generate negative word of mouth. So, it was better to just say no to all of them. I knew he was cognizant of the PR aspect, but I think to him, the inherent injustice of it— the idea of hurting some poor kid who was left out—was far more important.

We drove off and left the parallel-parking for another day.

9

Smells Like Good Stuff

A lot of the times in the late afternoon, Wilt and I would end up hanging out in my sister's room at the end of the hall, listening to music. Sybil had a nice record player and was never there. She was a sophomore at Temple University now and was out all the time.

Her room was in its own part of the upstairs. Wilt was in my room, and I was in the guest room right next to it. That was on one side of the house, along with the bathroom. Then there was a long hallway that went past a small sundeck on the roof, and Sybil's room was at the far end of the hall. It was a universe unto itself, and the door to that universe was always closed.

One thing I learned early in life is that you never, under any circumstances, entered her room without knocking first, and then you had to wait for her permission to come in. This was a cardinal rule and we all obeyed it implicitly. Only Geneva had free rein to come and go as she pleased.

Sybil was what was called a beatnik in those days. My mother just called her a "vilde chaya," which is a Yiddish term that doesn't translate perfectly into English, but basically means a "wild Indian." And that shoe really fit.

She was a lot like the weather in our part of the world—lots of warm, sunny days but some dark, stormy ones as well. And as her little brother, while I enjoyed basking in the sunshine when it was out, I always knew to get the hell out of the way whenever one of those storms blew through.

She was by no means a bad kid, adored her parents and was fiercely loyal to her family. But she had an untamable wild streak running through her. And no matter what was going on, she was always her own boss.

The first time I really saw it was during the 1960 presidential campaign. My father was for Nixon. He was tight with the Pennsylvania Republican party and had met both Eisenhower and Nixon. He had even run unsuccessfully for Congress in 1956.

On top of that, he was no fan of the Kennedys. In his view, Joseph Kennedy had been weak on Hitler during the war, and he didn't trust him when it came to Jewish welfare. And in my father's world, the apple never falls too far from the tree.

Sybil, on the other hand, fell madly in love with JFK. He was the first candidate who was a real media superstar, and my then fifteen-year-old sister was crazy about him. She pasted about five hundred pictures of him on her wall in a massive collage. I think my father got nauseous every time he saw it and avoided ever going into her room. Even after the election, her JFK shrine endured for quite a while.

Now that she was in college, her taste in wall décor had veered off into some new directions. One of her girlfriends was a talented portrait painter, who later became a famous courtroom artist. She painted three large full-color paintings for Sybil, who displayed them prominently in her room.

Two were portraits of Sybil. In one, she was wearing an enormous black-feathered hat. It looked like her head was covered by a dark, foreboding raven. In the other, she was seated on a big, comfortable gold easy chair, with an opened book lying face-down on her lap. From the sour look on her face, she was either the most bored or the most depressed person in the world.

But she hung the masterpiece of her collection in the center of the back wall, and it really grabbed your attention when you walked in the room. In the rear of the large painting was a blindfolded naked woman hanging from a meat hook by her tied hands. A priest stood in the foreground, dressed in a black suit and a black shirt with a white priest's collar. He was holding a Bible in his hands with a gold crucifix on top of it. And he was staring daggers at you.

Sybil added her own piece of art to the mix. She made a collage and put it right next to the painting. She covered a large piece of poster paper with cutout photos of every form of human suffering imaginable. It was unbelievably awful. And in the middle, she put a true-to-life depiction of Jesus on the cross.

She was obviously making a statement of some kind, but it probably would have gone over better in a dorm than in her room at home. My father couldn't stand it.

I was sitting with him in the kitchen having ice cream one Thursday night, while my mother was still in New York doing her charity work. Something seemed to be bothering him. The whole time we ate, he had a weird look in his eye, like his mind was on a slow simmer. Suddenly it exploded into full boil.

"God damn it!" he said and smacked his hand down on the kitchen table. He stood up, went over to a drawer, rummaged through it and pulled out a medium-size carving knife. "God damn it!" he repeated and angrily stomped out of the kitchen toward the steps that led upstairs.

"What the hell is this?" I thought and went running after him. Knife in hand, he ran up the steps, then down the hall to Sybil's closed door. He burst it open without knocking and flicked on the lights. I had no idea what he was up to, but I was glad she wasn't home.

He walked right over to her human suffering collage, and using the sharp point of the knife, started scraping off the Crucifixion scene. He attacked it like a maniac and kept going until he had gotten rid of every last bit of it. When he was finished, he stood there and stared at the poster for a moment. Then he turned around and looked at me. I had absolutely nothing to say, and neither did he.

Now, of course, symbols mean different things to different people, and whatever that image meant to him, he clearly didn't want it in his daughter's bedroom. But now it was gone, and everything seemed fine. We walked back to the kitchen together, sat down at the table, and finished our ice cream as though nothing had happened.

My mother was absolutely horrified when she got home later, and he told her what he'd done. Somewhat of an artist herself, she felt he had no right to invade Sybil's room and inflict his will on her creative expression. She thought it was appalling.

When Sybil got home the next day and my mother sheepishly began to give her the details, my sister made a point of being outraged. But her biggest effort was to hide her deep relief.

When my mother said, "Sybil, Daddy went into your room last night," her heart sank, and she got really scared. But when she heard what happened, she was so happy she almost burst out laughing, but kept a straight face.

She told me years later that she always kept an ounce of grass in the drawer of the night table next to her bed. She couldn't have cared less about the collage, but if he had found the marijuana, it could have been a disaster. She would have really had to reach into her bag of tricks to wiggle her way out of that one. We both knew she could have done it—she was that good. But it would have been quite a challenge, even for her.

Now, this was still the early days, when marijuana had just started blowing in the wind, and not too many people were smoking it at the time. But she had really gotten into it.

When she first started, I could clearly smell a pungent, unfamiliar odor in the air. It definitely was not the same as the normal cigarette smoke that pervaded every other part of our house. When I asked her about it, she told me she had begun burning incense. It was a new thing she had found, a study aid that would clear her mind and help her concentrate. It made sense to me.

One day, during Wilt's stay, she was home in her room with the door closed. Wilt and I were in my room, and I had to drive him somewhere. As we walked out into the hall, it reeked of that smell of hers. He immediately picked up on it and stopped on the landing before we went downstairs.

"What's that?" he asked me, taking a couple sniffs of the air.

"Oh, Sybil's into burning incense now. She does it all the time. It helps her study."

"Really?" Wilt said, sounding impressed. He looked at me like I was a five-year-old. "So, you think that's incense, huh?"

I didn't say anything. What else could it be?

"OK," he said with a chuckle. "Incense it is."

But before he moved, he took one more sniff and nodded in appreciation. "It smells like some pretty good stuff to me," he added, and we left.

10

Chances Are

A big back-to-back showdown was coming up with the Celtics. We'd play them at home in Convention Hall on Saturday night, March 6, with a game in Boston the following Sunday afternoon on national TV.

Every game between Philly and Boston was a major battle and to this day, it's still seen as one of the greatest sports rivalries of all time. Some people think it was a contest between Wilt and Bill Russell, but that's only part of the story. Russ was a great player, but one-on-one, he was no match for Wilt. Nobody was.

It was Wilt against the entire Celtics organization, from the brilliantly cunning coach, Red Auerbach, all the way down. They were a well-oiled machine, had won nine of the past ten NBA championships, and when they played us, they had only one key strategy: to take down Chamberlain.

March 6 was my brother's twenty-fourth birthday, and we celebrated at the game. He and his wife, my mother, Sybil and I sat in our usual seats under the basket. My father sat right next to the bench, about twenty-five feet to our right. Gotty, as always, sat next to him.

From the instant the players appeared, the scene was unbelievably intense, with ten thousand screaming fans on top of every play. The teams fought each other tooth and nail, and at halftime, we had a one-point lead, 55–54.

Physically, it had been a brutal game. But once the second half started, it became outright warfare. The Celtics were triple-teaming Wilt with their crew of skilled hatchet men—tough guys who knew how to play dirty. They leaned on him, pushed him and hit him with their elbows whenever the refs weren't looking. With the crowd crazier than ever, we had a slim lead at the end of the third quarter, 75–73.

When the fourth started, the place was a madhouse, and the game kept getting rougher. At one point, Wilt and Russell started mouthing off to each other and seemed almost ready to come to blows. Then a moment later, Celtics bruiser Tommy Heinsohn threw a punch at Wilt.

Heinsohn was a great player but he was also a notorious hatchet man and had been dishing it out to Wilt all night. At one point, he shoved Wilt. Wilt pushed back and turned to take his position under the basket. As he did, Heinsohn punched him in the shoulder. Wilt turned around with his right hand clenched in a fist. Both benches immediately emptied out onto the floor, and the refs scrambled frantically, trying to stop a major brawl. It was the only time I ever saw Wilt ready to hit someone.

Now we all hated every Celtic player, but Heinsohn was public enemy number one, with his own personal pedestal in the Philadelphia hall of villains. He had blindsided Wilt, punching him while his back was turned, and the fans went ballistic. They sounded like a violent, angry mob and I had never heard such rage in a crowd before. It was blood-curdling.

There was an automatic time-out and things finally calmed down a little. But as soon as play resumed, it was obvious that the game was over. You don't do that kind of thing to Wilt Chamberlain in front of his hometown crowd and then go back to business as usual. The fans demanded revenge and he was more than happy to give it to them.

He took command of the floor and the whole 76ers team went into a different level of play. We quickly built up a strong lead and ended up winning fairly easily. Following the satisfying victory, the euphoric crowd began to file out.

***

Mike and his wife said good-bye, and Sybil was itchy to go as well.

"Mom, can we leave as soon as Dad comes out?" she asked. "I've got a bunch of stuff to do." She didn't come to the games that much anymore. She had come tonight for Mike's birthday.

"Hold on for a few minutes," my mother said with a slight smile. "I think someone may be coming by to meet you."

"Oh great," Sybil said sarcastically. She turned to me and muttered that there was some distant cousin who had started going to Temple, and our parents wanted Sybil to show her around. "God, I hope I don't have to meet that creep tonight," she said impatiently.

Gotty walked over and sat down next to my mother, who pulled out her knitting needles and started going at it. They launched into one of their Yiddish conversations. My sister and I sat there for a few minutes and off in the distance, a small group of men emerged from the back.

As they got closer, I could see Wilt walking next to

another tall guy that was Bill Russell. There was another black guy walking with them who was much shorter. And separately, a few yards behind, my father was walking with a man who could have been his double. He was just as bald, about the same size, and also dressed in a suit and tie.

As they got closer, I could see the other man was Red Auerbach, the Celtics coach. They went a few rows up into the stands and sat down on the aisle. My father handed him a cigar, and they both lit up. He always referred to Red by his real name, Arnold. They had known each other a long time and were fraternity brothers. Different schools, different chapters, but my father always called him "my brother, Arnold."

Wilt, Bill Russell, and this other guy came walking toward my sister and me.

"Sybil!" Wilt called out to her. "Syb, c'mere. I want you to meet someone."

Sybil looked at Wilt and then past him to Bill Russel and the other guy. Suddenly, an awestruck look came over her, and almost in a trance, she stood up and walked toward them. I trailed behind to see what was happening.

"Johnny Mathis," Wilt said as he put his hand on the guy's shoulder. "Say hello to Sybil Richman. She's a big fan." There was silence for a second. "Syb, Johnny is an old friend of Russ's from college, back in San Francisco."

He nodded at Russell, who stood there smiling at her stunned expression. "Maybe somebody should get her some water," he said to no one in particular.

Johnny Mathis was an enormous singing star at the time. His hit records had sold millions, and his silky voice had been a constant presence in Sybil's room. He was in town performing at the Latin Casino, the area's top local nightclub.

Now, Wilt and Russell were really cool-looking guys,

but it was a hip, casual, athletic cool. By contrast, Johnny was an entertainment superstar, and he really looked the part, perfectly groomed and magnificently dressed. And although he played it down, he was one star who really knew how to shine out in public. He gave Sybil a warm smile and turned on the charm. It was truly impressive, and she was truly impressed.

In addition to his musical talents, Mathis was also quite an athlete. He was a track star at San Francisco State around the same time that Wilt went to the University of Kansas. And that gave them a lot in common because when it came to sports, track was really Wilt's first love.

Besides playing basketball for Kansas, he had also been a major star on its track team. He won the conference high jump championship three years in a row and competed at the top collegiate level in the broad jump, shot put, one-hundred-yard dash, quarter-mile, and half-mile runs. He loved track because it was largely an individual sport, so his success was much less dependent on the performance of his teammates or just plain luck.

It turned out that my father had set up Sybil's meeting with Johnny, after hearing he was coming to town. He told Wilt, who then called Bill Russell. Despite their fierce rivalry on the court, Wilt and Russ were good friends and had tremendous respect for each other.

Also, the owner of the Latin Casino was either a friend or client of my father's, probably both. I first heard about his nightclub connection when I was in third grade. The Three Stooges were coming to play at the Latin and my parents were thinking of having a birthday party for me there.

"I'll ask Dave Douchoff to have Lewy Feinberg give me a call," my father said, one Saturday afternoon during lunch.

"Who the hell is Lewy Feinberg?" my mother asked.

"Oh, he's from the old neighborhood. His parents lived a few blocks away from Mom and Pop. Goes by the name of Larry Fine now. He got in with these two brothers, Moses and Jerry Horwitz, and they formed an act. That's who the Three Stooges are. Curly, Larry, and Moe are really Horwitz, Feinberg, and Horwitz."

"Sounds like a law firm," my mother said dryly as she cut the rye bread.

"Yeah. And they'd be a lot better than some of the clowns out there now, running around pretending to be practicing law."

I couldn't believe my ears. The news that the Three Stooges were Jewish absolutely staggered me. Although I loved them, their moronic style of slapstick humor seemed a little too lowbrow to be coming down the same rarified pipeline that brought us the Torah and the Talmud. Still, for some strange reason, it suddenly made me feel a little better about having to go to Hebrew School.

We saw the show and it was great. Afterward, Dave, the owner, took my father and me backstage to the dressing room for autographs. He warned us that it was going to be quick. It had been a matinée, and this was the last day of the run. They had a train to catch to New York, where they were opening tomorrow.

When we walked into the room, I kept looking around, but I didn't see the Stooges anywhere. Finally, Dave introduced us to these three guys and said they were Curly, Larry, and Moe.

Like most men in those days, they were each wearing wide-brimmed fedora hats. As I concentrated on their faces, I could tell that it really was them. But with these hats on, they looked just like any other Jewish guys my father's age. They could have easily been relatives at our cousin's club. They were in a huge hurry and didn't have a minute. They signed their group picture, and that was it.

I was shocked. The Three Stooges—these zany characters living in this wacky, cartoon-like world—were actually three normal middle-aged men, with regular worry lines mapped across their everyday Jewish foreheads.

I thought about them as I looked at Johnny Mathis. I had no problem recognizing him—he looked exactly like he did on his album covers. He and Sybil were off in their own world, beloved idol and adoring fan basking in the pleasure of each other's company. It was nice to watch.

Wilt and Russell slinked off and stood near the stands. They had their own private club and they were the only two members, speaking in clipped, ultra-hip phrases that only they understood.

My mother and Gotty were still sitting over in our seats, talking Yiddish and laughing a lot. As usual, she kept up a furious pace with her knitting needles.

I had nothing to do, so I walked over to the 76ers' bench, sat down, and took in the scene. My father and Red Auerbach sat in the stands puffing away on their cigars, engulfed in a cloud of white smoke, illumined by the bright lights.

Wilt and Russell and my father and Red were all so relaxed, you'd never know that a half hour earlier, they had been at each other's throats, and a vicious fight had broken out in front of 10,000 screaming maniacs. Tomorrow afternoon, they'd be going at it again, but this time in front of millions of fans on TV.

Suddenly, the big arena lights shut off, leaving only the house lights on. The maintenance crew got started and I heard the familiar sounds of them breaking down the wooden chairs and sweeping up the floor. The haunting echoes began reverberating throughout the empty hall. Those sounds were deeply ingrained in my being and always soothed me. We had been doing this since I was a baby and I used to fall asleep to them. I had been around for the breakdown and the cleanup since before I could remember.

The next afternoon, in retribution, the Celtics blew us out of the Boston Garden on national TV. It was close for the first quarter, but that was the end of it. By halftime, they were up by 19 and coasted along, killing us by 22.

It seemed that no matter what happened anywhere else, they were always invincible in The Garden. God only knows what it would take for us to ever be able to beat them up there.

11

Rev It Up, Ringo

Normally, whenever he got the chance, Wilt would have Archie drive him up to New York, so he could go hang out at his nightclub in Harlem. Philly had long ago become way too small for him. But with the playoffs approaching, my father ruled it out. He wanted to keep him close.

Most nights, the two of them would spend an hour or so together in my father's office on the first floor while I was doing my homework. Then, Wilt would come upstairs and goof around with me for a while. I'd always go to sleep at eleven o'clock. I have no idea what he did after that. He was a renowned insomniac, but he always said he never slept better in his life than he did in our house. And he was sound asleep every morning when I left for school.

One night, he came upstairs after being with my father. We both got down on the floor and started into our regular, unending game of War.

"Wanna know what kind of guy your father is?" he asked me as he was shuffling the cards. "He had the sports page opened when I walked into the office tonight, and he pointed to a picture in the paper and said, 'You know what Mickey Mantle did last weekend? He spent all day

Saturday and all day Sunday in a sporting-goods store, signing baseballs. And you know why he did that? He did it because he's broke. He drank and gambled all his money away. And now he's gotta spend his weekends doing this. Trust me, Wilton, when you're forty, you're not going to be signing basketballs for rent money.'" We started mindlessly playing our card game and he added, "He's got me buying land in Los Angeles now."

***

A few days later, in the afternoon, I was listening to a new Beatles album called Beatles '65. Like most of the kids in my generation, the Beatles were the absolute center of my world. I was beyond a fan, I was a devotee.

I had also fallen into a piece of genetic good luck: I had a beautiful head of Beatles hair, and I wore it just like they did. It never hurt to resemble the Fab Four in those days, and the look was a real plus when it came to attracting girls.

Unfortunately, though, I knew my run as a Beatles look-alike was going to be short-lived because my mop-top probably wasn't going to last all that long. I had first heard the bleak news when I was about eight and my father had taken me to the barbershop.

"Oh, he'll lose his hair early," the barber said as he started working on me. "He'll be totally bald by the time he's twenty-five."

I couldn't believe it. I looked at the barber, who was bald and then looked at my father, who was bald, then thought of my grandfather, who was also bald. I think that was the first time I understood that the genetic deck was clearly stacked against me. I felt doomed. The concept of losing my hair was absolutely appalling.

But after another few minutes, I figured—hey, the barber could be wrong—he's not God. Well, as it turned out, he wasn't God, but he was a pretty good prophet. By the time I was twenty-five, his vision of my future had been fulfilled in spades.

Anyway, back then, I still had the Beatles hair and I loved their new album. But there was one song that kind of surprised me, "I'm a Loser." In the verse, John Lennon kept singing – "I'm a loser. I'm a loser. And I'm not what I appear to be."

Now of all the superstars of the day, John was the ultimate. With all his fame and fortune, nobody seemed to have it better. So, what was with this song? I knew it was about a lost romance, but it sounded deeper than that. I heard an ache in his voice, like he really meant the words.

"Nice song," I heard Wilt say over the music. I looked up as he ducked under the doorway and walked into the room. He picked up the album cover and looked it over. The four Beatles were in a studio, dressed in suits and sitting under opened umbrellas.

"Not the most macho guys in the world," he said. "Look at their hair. They look like they just got out of the beauty parlor."

I looked up at Wilt, leaning against the wall with his head a few inches from the ceiling. At 7'1", with 300 pounds of pure muscle, he was definitely quite a contrast from the "Lads from Liverpool" pictured on the album cover.

"It looks good on you though," he said, reaching down and tousling my hair, which I immediately put back in place. After that, he started calling me Ringo from time to time.

A few nights later, I was going to drive him home after a game and we were in the Convention Hall stage door parking lot. We got in the car, and I started it up. "Wait a minute," he said. "Something's wrong. The motor doesn't sound right." We sat there listening for a few seconds.

"Do you hear that?" he asked. I didn't hear a thing.

"You know what? Pop the hood and let me jump out and take a look."

'What?" I asked.

"Yeah. I'm telling you, this thing doesn't sound right." He opened his door. "Don't worry. I'm a real mechanic."

I pushed the hood release, he got out and started checking the motor. As I sat behind the wheel, with the hood up, there was a crack at the bottom that was big enough that I could look through. I could see him from his waist to his chest.

Suddenly, a woman with a perfect body came over to him. I couldn't see above her shoulders, but I could see them embrace and they obviously started making out.

"Oh, I think I see what the problem is," he shouted to me, like he was working on the car. "Let's just let it run for a couple of minutes and see what happens."

He went back to making out with the woman, and things were quiet for a while as the motor ran. "OK, rev it up, Ringo," he finally shouted to me again. "C'mon. Give it a little gas."

I did, and we continued to play that game for about ten more minutes. The lady finally left, and he jumped back into the back seat.

"It sounds good now. I think I fixed it," he said with a satisfied smile. I pulled out and headed for home. "I'm great under the hood. You just have to know your way around in there."

***

The next night, as we were on the floor playing cards, we started talking about his experiences with women. At one point, I mentioned that he never had a steady girlfriend.

"What are you, observant now, man?" he asked me. Although his tone was a little on the sharp side, I could tell he didn't really mind. I didn't say anything. I knew how that part of his life worked. He was surrounded by an unending swarm of groupies and they were coming at him constantly. Sex was never a matter of if. It was just who, when, and where.

And he had made up his mind long ago that he would never get married. He knew he couldn't have a regular life with a wife and kids. His world was like a constant circus and there was just too much going on. And it never stopped. With all of its tumult and excitement, he knew he was destined to live a solitary existence.

"I will tell you one thing, though," he said, as he dealt a new hand. "There is someone I could see myself getting serious with." He stood up and walked over to his wallet. Whenever he got up, I was always surprised by how tall he really was, and that I had forgotten all about it.

He got back down on the floor, took out a black-and-white picture, and handed it to me. A blond woman was coming out of the ocean on a deserted beach. She was absolutely gorgeous. And she was absolutely naked.

At first, she looked like Marilyn Monroe, but it clearly wasn't her. Still, she was definitely familiar. I tried to make out her face, but my attention kept drifting to some of her other features.

"Don't you know who that is?" he asked me.

"Yeah," I said. "I mean, I know the face, but I can't put a name to it."

"It's Kim Novak."

"Oh, right!" I said. "Of course, it's Kim Novak. Wow. I see it now." And I did. It was clearly her and it was a huge deal. She was one of the top movie stars in Hollywood, and along with being a talented actress, she was also one of the hottest sex symbols on the planet.

He launched into an intimate, rapturous story about her. According to him, they were involved in a long-standing love affair. And she wasn't only unbelievably attractive and brilliantly talented, she was also one of the coolest people he had ever known.

He told me about a trip they had taken up to Muir Woods to walk together in the redwood forest. It was the only place he had found where he could go out in public and just be a normal person. He didn't have to deal with fame, and it was truly liberating for him.

After all, he wasn't a regular celebrity who could just put on a hat and sunglasses and walk around undisturbed. Wherever he was, if he stood up, he was Wilt Chamberlain and he couldn't disguise himself no matter what he wore.

In general, he loved being Wilt Chamberlain, but he always hated it when it was forced on him. And a lot of his life was filled with people gawking at him and saying inane things like—How's the weather up there? Hardly anyone ever spoke to him as a real human being. Instead, they basically treated him like a freak. And it could really wear on him.

But among the redwood trees, it was different. Hundreds of feet tall, next to them, he was nothing. His size was irrelevant, and nobody even noticed him up there. He was free from it all. His trip with Kim had been one of the best times of his life.

"She's really something else," he said to me and gazed out the window into the night. I couldn't help feeling a little sorry for him, and it wasn't the only time. When you're caught in a trap, the trappings don't matter. Despite all the fame, fortune and success, caught is caught and trapped is trapped.

12

Behind the Curtain

On Sunday, March 21, we played the Baltimore Bullets in the last game of the regular season and we beat them soundly by 22 points. My father was happy, the team was confident, and the playoffs were about to begin.

In the first round, we faced the Cincinnati Royals. They were a tough team with a powerful combination of two major stars: Oscar Robertson and Jerry Lucas, and they had the home-court advantage.

Game 1 was up there on Wednesday, March 24. It was brutal and went into overtime. At the last second, one of our guys threw up a Hail Mary, and it went in just as the twenty-four-second clock went off. There were all kinds of protests about it, but the refs said it was good, and we came home with the win. We had stolen the home-court advantage.

Unfortunately, we gave it right back on Friday, when they beat us in Convention Hall by one. Robertson and Lucas shot the lights out at the end of the game, and they squeezed out a 121–120 win.

We went back out there for a Sunday-afternoon game. Again, it was tooth-and-nail through three quarters, but our guys broke it open toward the end, scoring 13 straight points and winning by 14. So, we had won 2 out there, and they had won 1 in Philly. All three were away-game wins, which was unusual.

Wilt slept out for a few nights during that series, but he came back to our place on Monday morning to relax for a while. The next game was Wednesday night.

He would rather have gone up to New York, but my father said it was out of the question. It was only a five-game series, and this was our chance to wrap it up. We didn't want to have to go back to Cincinnati tied at 2-2 and try to beat them on their home court.

During those two days, Wilt was as cool and relaxed as ever. You would have never known anything was on the line at all. He went out walking, we drove around a few times, shot some baskets, and played a bunch of cards.

Wednesday afternoon, the day of the big game, I was supposed to drive him to the hall. My father called and told me to let Wilt know he needed to see him before the game. They were in the middle of one of their deals, and he had some papers for him to sign.

Around six o'clock, I grabbed a quick sandwich while Wilt was upstairs, packing. If we won, Archie was going to drive him up to New York for some fun. He'd have a few days off before the finals started, which would be against the Celtics. They had already clinched their spot.

We jumped in the car and headed to Convention Hall. We got there at about six-thirty, long before any of the crowd started to arrive. There was a guarded driveway next to the hall that led around back to the stage entrance. As soon as the guard saw the car, he recognized it and pulled the barrier away.

"Stop here for a second," Wilt said to me. He put down his window and looked at the guard. "Hey, Charlie, how you doin'?"

"Pretty good, Dipper," the guard said. "Pretty good, all things considered."

"Yeah, OK," Wilt said. "OK. So how is Doris doing?"

"Oh, she's hangin' in there, Wilt. Hangin' in. She's hangin' in and hangin' on." They looked at each other silently for a moment.

"All right, well, you be sure to tell her I was asking for her, and give her my best, will you?" Wilt said.

"I will. Thanks, pal. It'll mean a lot to her. And have a good one in there tonight. Bring it home, Big Guy!"

"Well, we'll do our best," he responded. "You know that's all we can ever do. You take care now."

I drove around back and parked near the stage entrance. I found out later that the guard was the brother of one of Wilt's close friends. He needed work, and between Wilt and my father, they got him that security job. Unfortunately, his wife had cancer and was in really bad shape. She only lived another month or so.

When we went inside, Wilt went upstairs to the team's locker room. Convention Hall was a performance venue with a huge stage. The basketball court was set up in the middle of the floor, with the stage at one end. The teams' locker rooms were converted dressing rooms on the second floor.

Downstairs behind the stage, there was an area that had a piano, a conductor's podium, a small desk, and a few chairs. I sat down on one of the chairs and waited for my father to get there. In that back area, everything was shut off by a thick, dark-blue curtain. It was kind of dark and very quiet. You could easily lose track of where you were.

"Hey, Shortstop," my father said to me. I hadn't heard him come in, and he startled me. "Wilt upstairs?" he asked.

"Yeah," I said.

"Did you tell him about meeting me here to sign the papers?" I nodded as he put his briefcase down on the desk. He was still in his lawyer role. He wouldn't become the team's owner and general manager for a few more minutes. In reality, basketball was just a sideline for him. It was all part of something much bigger, and like an admiral, his law practice was his captain's deck.

As an attorney, he always dressed perfectly for the part, with a freshly pressed suit, shined shoes, and manicured fingernails. "When you walk into a room, a courtroom, or anywhere else, the first thing they do is look at your shoes," he used to tell the younger lawyers in the firm. "If they're not shined, they think you're not thorough. You look like you don't pay attention to details. They probably don't even realize they notice it, but believe me, they do.

"Same thing with your nails. When you hand them a contract, and your fingernails are dirty, they can't help but wonder, 'What else about you might be dirty?'"

Every Friday afternoon, he used to spend a few hours at the men's club in the Broadwood Hotel downtown, around the corner from his office. He would take a steam, followed by a shower. Then, he'd go up to the barbershop for a haircut and a manicure. In those days, a lot of professional men used to wear shiny, clear nail polish.

He'd finish up his week that way, and then he'd be home early for Sabbath dinner. At synagogue the next day, he used to point out the Hebrew words to me in the prayer book, and I always made a game of trying to read the letters upside down as they reflected off his perfect nails.

He put his briefcase down on the small table and flipped on the lamp. Then he took out a couple of folders, pulled out some papers that looked like contracts, and opened them to the signature pages. I started to hear some dull murmurings coming from the other side of the curtain, but I was only faintly aware of them. "There," he said to me.

Soon, the guys on the team came down the steps, in single file. They were dressed in their 76ers warm-up suits and stood by the opening of the curtain. Wilt was last and stepped over to the desk, where my father was standing. They started talking about a few things—who was buying what, where, when, and for how much.

The guard pulled the curtain back a bit, and the other guys went trotting out to start their lay-up drills. The curtains were so thick, I could barely hear the applause. A few moments later, some dull murmurings began out there as well.

My father was talking to him, but I could see that Wilt wasn't really paying attention. His eyes were on the curtain, and his head was already in the game. Like a champion racehorse who was saddled-up and in the stall, he was ready to go. I could almost feel the adrenaline racing through his veins.

My father kept pointing to the signature lines and Wilt kept signing, barely looking at them. Eventually, my father put everything back in the folders, closed his briefcase, and gave Wilt a nod. Wilt walked over and stood next to the guard at the curtain. My father turned off the desk lamp and it got pretty dark. We walked over and stood a few feet behind Wilt.

He rose up on his tiptoes a couple of times and stretched his calves. Then he rolled his head around and loosened his neck and shoulders. He stood there for a few more seconds; then nodded to the guard, who parted the curtain.

A bright light burst in, and Wilt stood in it with

his hands on his hips. Within seconds, ten thousand fans jumped to their feet and started going crazy. The burst of light and the roar of the crowd completely surprised me. It had been so quiet backstage, I had forgotten where we were and that there was a big crowd out there.

Wilt slowly trotted out and my father and I walked a couple of feet behind him. The mass explosion of joy from the crowd was so powerful it pushed me backward and almost lifted me off my feet. I had never felt anything like it before.

As I took my seat and thought about it, I understood what had happened. When the rest of the team had come out and Wilt wasn't with them, the fans had gotten anxious. There had been no announcement and they were afraid he wasn't going to play for some reason. So, the murmuring I had heard backstage was everyone talking about it.

Suddenly Wilt appeared, healthy and strong, and the crowd erupted into an enthusiastic standing ovation. As we followed him out to the court, the energy directed his way was so powerful, it was like walking on air.

As the warm-up continued, I flashed back on the scene I had just witnessed between the two giants of their realms, my father and Wilt. The bond of trust between them was always so natural, I took it for granted. But watching Wilt sign those contracts just on my father's say-so, barely looking at them, drove home how deep their trust in each other really was.

The game was a runaway from the start. Wilt was unstoppable. He scored 38 points, grabbed 26 rebounds, and blocked 10 shots. The other guys were spectacular as well. We won it by 7, going away. There was a celebration in the locker room with champagne, and then Wilt disappeared. He went right up to New York to party in the big leagues.

In a couple of days, it would be time to try to do the impossible—take this ragtag team that Wilt had joined only two months earlier, and try to knock off the mighty Boston Celtics, the reigning NBA champions for the last six years.

13

Grand Larceny

Before we knew it, the finals began and for the next ten days, we went to war against Boston for the NBA Eastern Division title. It was a seven-game series. The winner would go on to play for the world championship. Every game was sold out, and every fan was going crazy at every single play. The air was charged with so much tension, you could hardly breathe.

The first game was up in Boston and was a total disaster. The Celtics ran away with it from the very beginning, and they beat us easily by 10.

They came back to Philly, trying to gain the major advantage of being up two games to none, but we pushed back hard and beat them by 6. We went back there, and they beat us by 8. Now they led 2 games to 1.

Game 4, back in Philly, became a "must win" for us. If we beat them, we'd be tied at 2 games each. But if they won, they'd be on their way back to Boston with a 3-1 lead, which would be nearly insurmountable.

It was a crazy game. We killed them in the first quarter and were up by 9. But they took it back in the second and went into halftime with a 5-point lead, 56–51.

With our fans agonizing over every play, the second half was fought point by point, with incredible ferocity, and it ended tied in regulation. During overtime, the Celtics tried desperately to put us away, but our guys stood strong, and we finally squeezed out a 3-point win.

Then there was a quick, even exchange. We went back to Boston, and they beat us by 6 and they returned to Philly, and we beat them by 6. So, the series was tied 3 – 3. With the exception of the very first game, each one was an even battle, climaxed by a brutal, second-by-second fight to the finish. Now it was time to go back to Boston for game 7, the final showdown, the grand finale.

It was a Thursday night; the game was on national TV and the odds were against us. In Philly, the whole city had come to a stop. For me, the whole world had come to a stop. This was it. Everything was on the line.

When the game began, it looked like the Celtics were going to blow us away. At the end of the first quarter, they had us by 9. But we came back at them like a team possessed and, amazingly, outscored them by 10 in the second quarter. We went into halftime hanging on by a thread, with a one-point lead: 62 -61.

But then, Boston Garden filled up with that old black magic of theirs, which meant nothing but poison for us. They dominated the floor, and by the time the fourth quarter began, they were up by 8.

As the final quarter unfolded, no matter how hard we tried, we just couldn't crack it. There was a small amount of give-and-take, but with only a little more than a minute left, the Celtics were still up by 7 and the game was basically over.

With that kind of team, having that kind of lead on their home court, I'm sure that they had the champagne on ice and were ready to pop the corks.

But Wilt went ballistic. He blocked 2 shots, grabbed 2 rebounds, and scored 6 points, accounting for all of the team's last 10, finishing it off with a decisive slam dunk. And suddenly, after his amazing flurry, we were only down 1.

But Boston still had the lead, and it was their ball with only 5 seconds left. All they had to do was put the ball in play and run out the clock.

Bill Russell grabbed the ball and went to make the inbound pass, but we went into an intense full-court press, and Russ couldn't find an open man. Out of time, he tried to make a desperate pass and the ball hit a temporary guide wire that was there to hold up the backboard.

It was an automatic turnover and a huge mistake on Russell's part. Now suddenly, we had the ball under our own basket with a full 5 seconds left! We immediately called a time-out and got ready for the big play. This was it. Down 1, if we could hit a field goal, we'd win the game and the series. With just one foul shot, we could tie it and send it into overtime.

The play was for Hal Greer, our superb point guard, to throw the ball into Chet Walker, our cool power forward. He had a super-smooth jump shot and would go for the win. Wilt would stake his position under the basket to grab the rebound and stuff it in if Chet missed.

But the Celtics had this one guy, John Havlicek, who went on to be their all-time leading scorer. A renowned competitor, he was a tremendous player, both offensively and defensively. On top of that, he was the true embodiment of the Celtic ideal, giving it 110 percent all the time. And like every other die-hard Philly fan, I hated his guts.

As they all lined up for the inbound pass, Havlicek placed himself strategically between Hal Greer and Chet

Walker. He figured the pass would be going to Chet, but he faked it and laid back, seeming to leave him open. Once Hal got the ball, he would have 5 seconds to throw it in, or it would be a turnover. When the ref handed it to him, Havlicek started counting in his mind: one-thousand-one, one-thousand-two, one-thousand-three, one- thousand-four. He glanced over his shoulder and saw Hal start to make the pass.

Then in a move of pure basketball genius, Havlicek jumped up in midair and gracefully intercepted the pass. He deflected it to a teammate and just like that, the game was over. And so was the series and our season.

It was one of the greatest defensive plays in American sports history and the entire Boston crowd flooded out onto the floor, mobbing their hero. They lifted him up on their shoulders and carried him around in triumph. Russell ran over and almost hugged the life out of him, grateful for resolving his mistake.

The announcer kept shouting deliriously as if he had lost his mind. "Johnny Havlicek stole the ball! It's all over! It's all over! Havlicek stole the ball! It's all over!"

And it was. As I vacantly stared at the euphoric celebration, it felt like the lifeblood was draining out of my body. I always knew we might lose. But the way it ended, with Wilt's epic performance wiped out by that cruel final blow, was a real killer. I was blindsided and went to bed drowning in a sea of misery.

I spent the next day in school in a morbid trance, like the walking dead. I didn't show it, but I felt like my insides had been kicked out. When I got home, I went straight upstairs. The door to my room was closed. I cracked it open. The curtains were drawn, and it was fairly dark, but it was obvious that nobody was there.

I flipped on the light and looked around. All of Wilt's

things were gone, and his side of the closet was empty. But his uniform was stretched out on the floor, right over the spot where we used to play cards.

I stared at his trunks and his huge jersey with the number 13 on it. I bent down to touch it, and it was still soaking wet with sweat from the night before. I got up, took a final look around the room, and left the house for a few hours.

When I came home for dinner and went up to my room, all the furniture was back to the way it was before Wilt came, and his uniform was gone. The two twin beds that had been tied together to make a double for him, had been separated and returned to their normal positions. I had my old room back and it was like nothing had ever happened.

My mother told me later that Archie had driven Wilt to the house straight from the airport that morning. He had packed up all his things and said good-bye.

I thought he had probably left his uniform there for me as a memento of our time together, but I'm sure my mother hadn't seen it that way. The team got new ones every year, so it would never be worn again. And the big memorabilia craze hadn't started yet, so a sweaty old uniform was nothing but trash.

I sat down on my bed and looked around. My room was back to normal and so was the rest of my life. The season was over. We had lost by a hair, the championship stolen away from us at the last second. Wilt's uniform was thrown away and he was gone. Along with my now-dead dreams of glory.

Part 2

14

A Coat of Many Colors

That evening, at Shabbat dinner, was the first time I saw my father since he came back from Boston. Every Friday night, my brother and his wife would join my sister, my parents and me at our house for the meal. The same two prayers were said, and the same dinner was served: Matzah ball soup, roasted chicken, and cherry or blueberry pie for dessert. My mother was a great cook, but only when it came to "real peasant food," as she called it.

Friday night dinner was an important tradition for us, sacred family time. My father took his relationship with God very seriously. His religion was more than just a formality to him - when he prayed, he meant it. And no matter what happened during the week, it was all left behind.

Still, I was expecting him to seem a little crushed or down in the dumps or something—anything. After all the 76ers, his creation, had just suffered an agonizing defeat. Instead, he looked like he didn't have a care in the world.

I didn't show my feelings, but I was still having a terrible time with the loss. On the surface, I was fine. But deep down, I was drowning in an ocean of anger and despair and couldn't let go of the inner turbulence.

The next morning, Saturday, as usual, we went to Temple Sholom, the synagogue in our old neighborhood, where we still belonged. My brother was away, so my father and I drove over alone. My mother and sister didn't have to go on Saturdays. They only went a few times a year, on High Holidays.

The synagogue, a Grecian-style temple with noble white columns and a large front portico, was built in the late 1940's. We were very active there and my parents were founding members. My father had been president twice, and my mother often chaired the Sisterhood.

We pulled up as usual, but as soon as I saw the building, I suddenly had to deal with my real feelings about God, given what had just happened, and it was like throwing gasoline on a fire. How could he have let the Celtics win like that? We couldn't have prayed any harder. Why did he let that happen? What's the point of all these prayers anyway? Is there really anybody up there?

Of course, I'd heard that God works in mysterious ways, but I wasn't buying it. It just seemed like a cop-out. If he really did exist, he was probably some kind of jerk. I knew my feelings were infantile, but my mind kept churning out a steady stream of putrid thoughts, like it was connected to a ruptured, polluted sewer pipe.

My father, on the other hand, was the exact opposite. All was well, as he calmly strolled into his spiritual home, ready to spend some quality time with his maker. And no one said a word to him about the loss. That was part of the outside world and had no place in here. Only the janitor said, "Tough one Thursday night, Mr. Richman. Too bad."

"Yeah," my father shrugged. "Hey, what are you gonna do?" And that was it.

We went in and sat down for the three-hour-long

service. For years, we had a deal that I could take a fifteen-minute break around the halfway point, when they started reading the Torah. It was my time-off for good behavior. My father would go up to the dais and join the rabbi and I could go out and take my break. I was supposed to be back in time for the end of the reading, when I would go up front and wait for him to come down the steps. Then we'd walk back to our seats together. It was our own little tradition.

At about 10:30, he went up to join the rabbi and I left. I went to the bathroom as usual, then started strolling around the place. Besides gorging myself on all the cookies, cakes, and pastries they served at the end, my break was always the high point of the morning for me.

I ended up in the big auditorium, which was already prepared for the after-service reception. As usual, I sat down near the back wall and stared up at the huge color mural that covered it, which highlighted seven episodes in the life of Joseph, a pivotal figure in early Judaism. I must have spent a total of a few hundred hours staring at it, because I usually had some extra time, and there was never anything else to do. By then I knew every crack in the paint.

But as always, I kept an eye on my watch to make sure I'd be back in time to meet my father when he came down the steps. I once learned how much our tradition meant to him when I was about ten minutes late and missed our walk back.

He was already sitting in his seat when I returned. As I passed him, he just kept staring into his prayer book, never raising his head. When I sat down and looked over at him, I couldn't believe how sad and disappointed he was. He looked like he was going to cry. He didn't say a word to me about it, but I never did that again.

This time, when I looked at my watch, I knew I was early and went back to staring at the mural of Joseph, which was disturbingly realistic. I was usually in there all by myself and it could get a little spooky. The characters looked so real, I felt like at any minute they might come alive and start talking to me. I guess I had seen too many Twilight Zones.

I knew all about Joseph from my religious studies, which were relatively strict. By a fluke, I had been trained as an Orthodox Jew. When we moved to the suburbs, my parents enrolled me in a place called Mikveh Israel, the oldest functioning synagogue in the United States.

It was orthodox, and even though we were more liberal, their suburban branch was only a mile from our house. It was very small, with only three kids in a class, and in that kind of environment, you really had to know your stuff. I got about eight hours a week of intensive Jewish instruction and prayer, so when it came to religion, they gave me a major dose.

Joseph's story always fascinated me, with so many twists and turns, it could have been a soap opera. He was his father's heir, but his brothers got jealous, betrayed him and sold him into slavery. He was taken to Egypt, where he worked for a wealthy army officer. The officer's wife repeatedly tried to seduce him, but he always refused her. Finally, infuriated by the rejection, she accused him of attempted rape. He was arrested and left to languish in prison.

But he was a gifted interpreter of dreams. The Pharaoh heard about it and summoned him to decipher a disturbing set of dreams he'd had. Joseph's interpretation was so astute that, recognizing his advanced wisdom, the Pharaoh not only pardoned him, but elevated him to royalty. Soon he made him the governor of the entire kingdom. And that's only the first act.

I was always attracted to the middle part of the mural. In one panel, Joseph is asleep, wearing the "coat of many

94

colors" his father had given him. He is having a dream, where his brothers are bowing to him. In the next panel, he is dressed as an Egyptian prince, from his gold crown down to his leather sandals. He is seated on a throne in front of the pyramids, and his brothers are bowing to him as well.

In the Bible story, when he woke up from his sleep as a young man, he had no idea what his strange dream meant. But years later, in real life, it all came true exactly as he had dreamt it. He did become a powerful prince in Egypt and his brothers did bow to him when they saw him. His unusual dream had actually been a prophecy.

I always liked these kinds of Bible stories, with psychic events, prophets, and miracles. They were like Twilight Zones from the ancient times. The other stuff, like who begat who, and who smote who, was pretty dry. And the political intrigue, along with all the battles just left me cold. You could read about that kind of thing any day in the newspaper.

But these metaphysical events were different. And the rabbis would hold long discussion groups about them, which were a welcomed relief from all the language repetition and constant memorizing. They would pose deep questions from old Jewish traditions of inquiry. What is the purpose of all this human drama? Why did we come here? Is there a deeper meaning behind it all? Besides our everyday identity, do we have a true self that doesn't change? Can God ever really be known, or do we have to just believe in him?

They were incredibly perplexing, and according to the ancient teachings, no one could answer any of it for you. You had to find it all out for yourself. As I sat there in the empty hall and stared up at Joseph sitting on his throne in the mural, I felt like I wanted to get out of there before he came alive, stepped down off the wall and started giving me his point of view. One thing I learned early about the Jews - everyone has an opinion and they're always ready to share it with you.

It was time for me to join my father anyway, so I went over, met him at the bottom of the dais and we walked back to our seats together. After another hour or so, services were over, and as usual, we went into the auditorium for the reception.

My father talked to a never-ending stream of fellow congregants, while I went straight to the refreshments: challah bread with honey, chocolate-chip cookies, brownies, and three different kinds of Danish pastries, all washed down with pure grape juice. The basic rule of the day was "All you can eat." And I always obeyed it religiously.

15

We're in the Black

Soon, it was time to leave and go visit my grandparents, my father's parents, who lived about a mile away from the synagogue. We always stopped in on our way home.

I had calmed down a little in services, but as we started walking to the car, that rowdy horde of negative inner demons came barging back into my mind like they owned the place. A wildfire of agitation burned through me, but I kept my mouth shut. Even so, I was pretty sullen by the time we started driving.

"What's the matter with you?" my father finally asked, bluntly.

"Nothing," I said.

"Nothing? You look like somebody died. What's the matter?"

"What? Are you kidding?" I answered, flabbergasted. He didn't say anything and kept driving. "We lost!" I finally blurted out, somewhere between shouting and bursting into tears. He was quiet for a few moments and kept driving.

"Duvid," he finally responded with a soft smile. "You're missing something."

We were about a block away from my grandparents' house. When we reached their corner, instead of parking the car, he kept driving.

"Do you know what you're missing?" he asked me.

I didn't answer. I didn't know, and I didn't care. I was far too demoralized and still just plain angry.

"Hey, come on, Shortstop," he said. "Open your eyes."

He reached over to me as he was driving, put his hand on my shoulder and shook me, like he was trying to wake me up. He stroked the back of my head for a second and then put his hand back on the wheel.

"OK, so we lost," he said empathetically. "And believe me, I'm just as upset about it as you are. Actually, I'm far more upset about it than you'll ever be. But you know what? Even though we got beat, we had a pretty good year. In fact, we had a great year."

He kept on driving aimlessly around the neighborhood. It was a beautiful mid-April day, and the promise of spring was everywhere.

"You know what the attendance was at Convention Hall Tuesday night?" he asked me. "Eleven thousand one hundred and eighty-two! And the place can't really hold ten thousand. We had to put up every folding chair we could find, and we sold nine hundred standing-room-only tickets. Do you hear that? Nine hundred people stood up for the whole game, and they paid to be there.

"Alright, they beat us, and that whole thing with Havlicek at the end was murder. But you're missing something, and it's important."

He pulled the car up to my grandparents' place, but we sat there with the motor idling. "Every single fan in the city is in love with the team now. And everybody from the mayor on down is just dying for the season to start next year. They can taste the championship and we're gonna sell out every game. They can't wait for Wilt to -"

"Dad, it's not gonna happen," I interrupted him. "Wilt's gonna quit. The newspapers say he's finished. He's definitely not coming back. It's over."

Wilt had always said that he was getting tired of playing basketball in the NBA and that he was sick of being the villain all the time. There had just been a controversial story about it in Sports Illustrated, and all three Philly papers covered it as well. The heartbreak in The Garden was the final nail in the coffin. My father just laughed.

"Wilt's not going to quit," he said. "There's no way in the world Wilt's going to quit." He turned the motor off. "That might be what he's saying right now. And you know what? That might even be what he's thinking. That might be what's in his mind, but that's not what's in his heart. Trust me, he's got a fire in him now that's bigger than he is, and he can't wait for next year. I guarantee you he's not going to quit." He turned and looked at me with a wise smile.

"Let me ask you a question. How many times since we got Wilt have I asked you to get your friends together and help me out at a game? How many times?"

He was referring to something I had completely forgotten about. It seemed like from another life. Before he made the trade for Wilt, attendance at 76ers games was awful. We were lucky to get two thousand fans into the ten-thousand-seat arena. He drafted a star player named Luke Jackson, and that picked things up a little. But we never drew more than five thousand. That meant half-full was the best we ever did. And half-full is half-empty, which was the way it always looked and sounded.

A born promoter, my father came up with endless gimmicks and tricks to try to get fans to come to the games. Free basketball night. Free T-shirt night. Buy one hot dog, get two free. Free date night.

He'd ask me to bring some friends to a game, and we'd spend the hour afterward giving all this stuff away— buttons, pins, banners, hats, balls, you name it. But it would always be a depressing scene. We'd end up with boxes and boxes that never got opened because hardly anybody ever came. None of his stunts ever worked.

"You don't remember the old days, do you, Big Boy? Well, you know something? Those rough old days were just a few months ago."

He was right. He had tried everything to get a foothold with the city's fans and failed miserably. Then, he pulled his magic rabbit out of the hat, and now we couldn't find enough chairs. Not to mention, we came within a hair of winning the championship. I was starting to see his point. Maybe it hadn't been that bad of a season after all.

"In two weeks, I'm going to sit down and negotiate the TV contract for next year," he continued. "The meeting's been on the calendar for six months. But guess what? What kind of position do you think we're in now?" He paused for a second. "Now—and pay attention to this— now I'm going to be talking about a three-year contract, not a year-by-year like before. And there's going to be a minimum guarantee in there. That would have been out of the question before Wilt. And it's the same thing when I talk to Convention Hall.

"And, also, think about this. Think about all the people who are going to have steady work now. The ticket sellers, the hot-dog guys, the trash guys, even the cabbies. There's going to be plenty of money flowing around next year. Plenty for everybody." He paused and looked at his watch for a moment.

"Now, listen to me, Duvid, and understand what I'm saying. We made it. We're in the black!" There was nothing more to say and we just sat there. "OK, kid, come on. Let's go inside and see Bubbe and Zayde."

He opened his door and I opened mine.

"Oh, right, this is a business," I remembered. Of course, I had always known it, but I had a deeper view of it now. I never looked at professional sports in quite the same way after his talk. He put his arm around my shoulder and we walked on.

"Wanna hear the secret of life in a nutshell?" he asked.

"Sure," I answered.

"Eat the nuts. Discard the shells."

He was a long-time member of Optimist International and loved pithy sayings like that, but I didn't pay much attention to it. Many, many years would pass before I began to appreciate the power of that simple insight of extracting the value of things.

16

We'll Do What We Have to Do

We went in for our usual half-hour visit with my grandparents, Bubbe and Zayde. They lived in the same two-bedroom apartment they had been in for my entire life. Walking through their door was like going back in time, into another world. Their place was exactly the same as it had always been. Nothing ever changed in there. Almost all the walls were covered with family pictures that went as far back as the 1890's. And it usually smelled like boiled chicken, a little on the stale side, but very comforting.

Although they were always thrilled to see me, most of the visits were one long Yiddish conversation between them and my father. As I sat there and listened, I couldn't help noticing the contrast between them.

He was one of the most respected attorneys in the city, a modern, successful American entrepreneur. And they, on the other hand, were very much from "the old country," a distant time and place that had nothing to do with the here and now, as far as I could see. In reality, my father was like a bridge between two worlds. And the way he built that bridge was truly remarkable.

As Americans, it's the same for all of us. Somewhere along the line, we each have relatives who have built it. We truly are a nation of immigrants, and unless you're one of the 2% who are Native American, your ancestors originally came here from somewhere else.

Every family's immigration story is individual and unique. Ours began in Philadelphia in 1912, when my grandparents first met. They were two impoverished immigrants, who had come here with virtually nothing. Each had to run for their lives, escaping the terrible brutality and violence that had erupted in their old homeland.

When they were introduced, he was twenty-two and she was just fifteen. They got married relatively quickly, and she gave birth to my father when she was still only sixteen. Their second child, a daughter, followed immediately on his heels.

Zayde, a former Yeshiva student, had to earn money immediately, so he put aside his religious aspirations and went into the wallpaper trade, learning how to be a paper hanger. After a few years, he was able to go out on his own and opened a paint-and-paper store in South Philly. Eventually, he and my grandmother bought the building and raised their family above the store.

It was a classic American refugee tale, and like most of them, it was only a small part of a much larger picture. In reality, they were in the second major wave of Jewish immigrants that hit the US shores.

The first one began around 1840. Before then, there were only about fifteen thousand Jews in the whole country. From 1840 to 1880, about 250,000 Jewish immigrants arrived, mostly from Germany. They were highly educated, well-to-do people, and became solid US citizens. Part of the American mainstream, thousands fought in the Civil War. They blended in with their new home and to a large degree, assimilated into the population.

But then, late in the 19th century, violent antisemitism broke out in Russia and Eastern Europe. More than a hundred thousand Jews were murdered in twelve hundred state organized massacres called "pogroms." The brutality was severe and over three hundred thousand Jewish children were orphaned.

The Jews had to run for their lives, and within thirty years, more than two and a half million of them flooded into the United States. Largely uneducated, penniless peasants who couldn't speak English, they had to struggle just to survive.

But they did far more than just survive. Amazingly, they flourished and had a tremendous impact on their new home. Usually with nothing but brains, talent, and sheer guts, these immigrants, and especially the generation that followed, became extremely successful doctors, lawyers, educators, scientists and businesspeople, making positive contributions to hundreds of communities across the United States.

And importantly, some of them went into show business, and they played a key role in creating the very character of America. With a major influence on literature, movies, radio, and TV, both onstage and off, they became a primary source of American music, comedy, and drama. In fundamental ways, their artistic contributions helped weave the fabric of our nation, shaping us into the people we are today.

My father was one of those extraordinary first-generation Americans. Living with his family above the paint and paper store, he went through a normal upbringing for the times, eventually going to South Philadelphia High School.

After graduating, he went on to Temple University, where he met my mother and they fell in love. During his last two years in college, he got friendly with a couple of lawyers. With their encouragement, he decided law might be a good profession for him.

Getting into law school back then was a little different than it is today. My father had a five-minute conversation with the dean, who told him to bring my grandfather in to meet him. When they met, the dean took one look at him and said, "Now listen, you have to understand something—While he's in law school, he's not going to be able to make any money. None whatsoever. He won't earn a thing. You're going to have to carry him for at least two years."

"Yeah, I know," Zayde said.

"You think you can handle it?" the dean asked.

"We'll do what we have to do," Zayde replied.

The dean looked at my grandfather for a moment. Then he turned and looked over at my father. "OK. You're in," he said and held out his hand. My father gave him a handshake and that was the end of it—or, more accurately, the beginning.

He and my mother were married in 1938 and they moved into my grandparents' house above the store with the rest of the family. They lived like that for a few years, until he made enough for them to be able to strike out on their own.

***

By the time I came along in 1949, they had gotten pretty far down the road. My father was a partner in his own law firm. And he was getting involved with professional basketball as well, through his former gym teacher from high school, Edward "Eddie" Gottlieb, who was known to the world as "Gotty". They would remain close associates and dear friends for life.

Born in Kiev, Gotty had come over to the United States as a child. He got into basketball in his early twenties, starting a team that played for the South Philadelphia Hebrew Association, called the Philadelphia SPHAs. Basketball in those days was mainly just the opening act for the Big Band dances that would be held as soon as the game was over.

Different leagues came and went, and Gotty was involved with most of them. In 1946, just after the war, he was the main force in starting a larger, more organized league. He and his friends wanted to give it a big name, so they called it the National Basketball Association.

He coached the Philadelphia franchise, the Warriors. They won the championship in the late 1940s, and in 1952 he bought the team. My father had been his attorney for years and executed the purchase. He also became General Counsel.

I was only three years old. So, for all intents and purposes, there was never a time in my life when professional basketball wasn't a major part of it. But only one part. This was America in 1952, and in a lot of ways, things were just getting started.

17

Be Strong Davy: Part I

The years that were to come laid the foundations not only for my father and the path he would take in his career, but for my character and the path I would take in my life. They shaped us both into who we became. And even though it's well over half a century ago, it's all still very fresh in my mind.

We lived in a neighborhood of row homes and were a typical family for the times—a husband and wife, two boys, one girl, a dog and a bird, and of course a television, which was still kind of new. Less than 35% of the homes in the country had one.

We watched it all the time and in my young mind, our world was an extension of what was on it. Our home life seemed like just another happy TV show. The times were ordinary, and I thrived on the normality of it.

The only unusual character in my life was my father's father, Zayde. Although he was still the patriarch of the extended family, by then, my father had assumed a lot of responsibility. Still, Zayde was the undisputed spiritual authority.

Spiritually, he certainly had his credentials. He had grown up in Lithuania as an orthodox Yeshiva student. A gifted singer, he was studying to become a cantor. In a Jewish service, the rabbi gives the sermon and leads the prayers, but the cantor is the one who sings them. And ideally, he should do it with so much feeling in his heart, the prayers go straight to heaven.

And Zayde could really do it, but he had to let it go when he came to America. His young wife had gotten pregnant, and he had to make a living. He still practiced his religion though, and his particular version was clearly on the mystical side.

You could see it when you looked at him. There was a twinkle in his pale-blue eyes and half the time, he looked like he was ready to burst out laughing. And the other half, crying.

Being who he was, he had some interesting theories about the cosmos. He said God was always pulling humanity closer and closer to him, and the new communication technologies—radio, movies, and TV, were all a part of it. None of them had existed in his early life, not even electricity. To him, they had been brought into being to help teach humanity profound lessons, elevating it to its highest potential.

And he also claimed there are highly evolved people living on Earth, to help bring about the Divine Plan. They're always here. In the ancient tradition, such a person was called a Kal-El, which means "vessel of God."

One day, to my delight, he decided that the TV character, the Lone Ranger, was such a one. It was a great development for me because he was the star of my favorite show, and if he had something to do with God, that was great. In my book, the show was a million times better than Hebrew school.

Zayde would watch each episode with total focus, and after it ended, he would give a short teaching on the moral of the story. One day, they showed an hour-long origin special about how it all began, and we watched it together.

The Texas Rangers were ambushed and left for dead by the bad guys. Tonto, the Ranger's future Indian companion, comes upon the scene, realizes that one of the rangers is still alive, and nurses him back to health. Since he's the sole survivor, Tonto calls him The Lone Ranger.

A few weeks later, they find a big white stallion lying near a bush bleeding to death, apparently gored by a bull. The Ranger and Tonto spend weeks caring for it. Once it fully recovers, they tie a rope around its neck and lead it into an open pasture.

"Your horse was killed, and now Great Spirit has given you a new horse," Tonto says, appreciating the synchronistic workings of the universe.

"He's not my horse yet, Tonto," the Ranger replies.

As they stand in the field, the horse feels its strength returning, and with its nose twitching, senses the call of the wild. The Ranger pats it on the head and slowly removes the rope. Then, he suddenly gives it a sharp slap on the rear.

The horse bolts forward and breaks into a mighty gallop, charging full speed to the top of a hill. It rears back on its hind legs, neighing in triumph, standing tall against the sky.

But when it comes back down on all four legs, a change comes over it. It tilts its head to one side, and then, as though sensing a call beyond the wild, it trots back over to the Lone Ranger and just stands there next to him.

"There, there, Big Fella," the Ranger murmurs to him, gently stroking its muzzle. Then he turns to Tonto, and in a voice of complete certainty says, "Now he's my horse."

The show went to commercial and Zayde turned to me, his face glowing like he had been staring at a burning bush.

"You see?" he asked me. "It's all about free will. God will never force you. He's just waiting for you to choose to be with him. You can do it whenever you want, but it's really up to you. God's in no rush. He has all the time in the world. And more."

Then, as always, he quoted some Hebrew or Yiddish phrase that I didn't understand. "You know what that means?" he asked me. I never did.

"It's simple. 'In the dark, you're blind. But in the light, you can see. Stand in the light and open your eyes.'" Then he touched the middle of my forehead with his index finger. "There's a light bulb in there. But it's up to you to screw it in and turn it on. Understand, Davy?"

***

Davy—now that was a magical name for me. To my grandfather, it was just short for Dave-a-lah, an endearing Yiddish nickname meaning "little David." But for me, it was the doorway into the realm of heroes.

I used to watch a TV show every afternoon called The Mickey Mouse Club. Probably every other baby boomer in the country with a TV did the same thing. It was our own private club, with a special membership cap that had mouse ears. Everyone seemed to have at least one.

There was a kindly uncle figure named Walt Disney, who ran the whole thing. With his deep voice of reason and benign authority, he came out and talked right to you. And there were magical creatures – like Jiminy Cricket who was the voice of conscience. And Tinkerbell, a fairy who could spread magic dust all around.

It was an enormously popular national phenomenon, but one day, they introduced a new character who took it to a completely different level. His name was Davy Crockett and he was The King of the Wild Frontier. It immediately became an unprecedented success and within weeks, Davy was the number one TV kids' hero in the country.

Disney launched a massive merchandising campaign that turned into a major profit center for them. The more popular the show got, the more stuff they sold. And the more stuff they sold, the more popular the show got. There was no end to it. I had three coonskin caps. Disney was selling over five thousand a week. I probably had six different styles of Davy Crockett T-shirts and a toy rifle, a replica of the one Davy always carried that he called Old Betsy.

Brave and light-hearted, always fighting for what was noble and right, Davy became the embodiment of the true American hero, and we all loved him.

But I got something a little extra. For me, all my life, I had always been called Davy. I was Davy Richman. Our new hero was Davy Crockett, and everybody called him Davy, as well. As if the line between fantasy and reality wasn't blurred enough already for me, now whenever I heard my name, I felt like a mythic hero. Every other six-year-old Davy in the country who was glued to a TV set probably felt the same way.

My life was deeply intertwined with Crockett's and I was having a great time, until the day my mother came home from the supermarket with a new comic book about him. It had great artwork, and I was enthralled by every part of it until I got to the end. The last few pages went into a dramatically realistic portrayal of Davy's death at the Alamo.

Disney had touched on the death briefly on TV but had just glossed over it, probably for advertising reasons. They didn't want you to feel too bad before their sponsors sold you candy and cereal, which was their bread and butter.

But this comic book was no Mickey Mouse job. The colors and the artwork were haunting, with noble, idealized writing. And unlike TV, it was static. It didn't move. You could just sit there and stare at it. Which I did, and it really brought the death alive.

They took you inside the Alamo, where Davy and his men were being defeated at every turn. One by one, all his companions are killed. Finally, Davy is surrounded by dozens of Santa Anna's soldiers, their bayonets bared, ready to tear him to shreds. Knowing he is out of ammo, he turns Old Betsy around, bravely swinging it in the air by the barrel, ready to go down fighting.

The last panel showed just his silhouette, swinging his rifle against the backdrop of a dark crimson sky. The caption read, "With no hope left, Davy fought on, and as the sky turned blood-red, The King of the Wild Frontier, the noble champion of truth, virtue, and all that is right, finally was no more."

I couldn't look away from that last panel. The color pictures saturated my mind and the truth sunk into me like a thousand-pound weight: Davy was dead. For the first time in my young life, I ran into the finality of death. And it took the life right out of me.

I closed the comic book and decided to go outside. I put on my favorite Davy Crockett T-shirt and my coonskin cap, picked up Old Betsy and walked out to our small front yard. Everything was the same as always, but I didn't know this world anymore. The light had gone out of it.

It was already late afternoon. I stood on our little hill and looked out at the sky. As the sun began to set, it turned blood-red, just like the end of the comic book. The deep color made my grief a hundred times heavier.

It was unbearable, and I closed my eyes and started to cry silently. Then, somewhere in the depths of my imagination, I thought I heard a deep voice talking to me from far away. "Be strong, Davy," it said. "It's time to be strong."

For a moment, I didn't know where I was. Then I heard another voice. "What are you doing?" it asked me. I realized it was someone in the real world.

I opened my eyes and saw my father standing there with his briefcase in his hand. He had just come home from work. He looked me over for a few seconds, dressed in my Crockett gear. I don't know if he was picking up on the fact that something profound had just happened to me, or if he was picking up on the fact that you could really move a lot of merchandise on TV. Whatever it was, he gave me a smile, picked me up, and carried me into the house.

As soon as we got in the hall, I smelled spaghetti sauce and knew we were having one of my favorite dinners. I immediately felt better. He said something to my mother in Yiddish and she started laughing—my favorite sound in the world. It made me feel even better than the spaghetti sauce.

18

Back to Reality

As I got a little older, I could never really understand what my father did for a living. I knew he was a lawyer, but I didn't know what that was. I knew what a doctor was and what a dentist did. My uncle owned a store and that made sense. But what in the world was a lawyer?

I figured it must have had something to do with helping people because he did that all the time. Same thing with my mother and her charity work. They were both compassionate people, especially when it came to our relatives. Sometimes, they'd give me a small role to play.

Once, we were having a family party at our house, and my father's cousin and his wife were coming. Although they had been trying for several years, she had been unable to get pregnant. This was the baby boom, and everyone was having kids. They were the only childless couple in the whole extended family and their chances weren't good. It was a real shame too because everybody knew they would be terrific parents, especially Cousin Elsie, who was born to be a mother.

She had a real fondness for me, and my mother always told me to be especially nice to her. I used to sit on her lap, and she'd tell me stories or read me a book. She always had a sweet smile, but I could sense a quiet sadness not too far beneath it. In her own way, my mother had made the situation clear to me, and in my own way, I understood it completely.

At this party, Cousin Elsie was bringing me a special gift. My mother said that when I opened it, whether I liked it or not, I should make a big deal about it, and be sure to thank her a lot.

About midway through the party, my mother called me into the kitchen to be alone with her and Elsie. After talking for a minute, Elsie brought out a big present wrapped up with a bow. When I opened it, something funny must have come out of my mouth, because they both started laughing.

I was a precocious little guy and used to say funny things without knowing it. At one Seder, my grandfather asked us all a question. "If there were only three founding fathers in Judaism, how come there were four founding mothers?" He went around the table. When he got to me, I said, "I don't know. I guess one of them was a bigamist."

Everybody thought it was a riot, but I didn't mean to be funny. We had just learned the word in vocabulary that week, and it seemed perfect. "Don't worry, Duv," my mother said. "We're not laughing at you. You just obviously got your father's legal mind."

This time with Elsie and my mother, they both got a good laugh. "You're so funny," Elsie said as she bent down and picked me up. "Oh, Davy, I love you."

She held me tight and kissed me on the cheek. Then, out of nowhere, she burst into tears. She kept rocking me, while she sobbed from the depths of her soul.

I felt sorry for her and wanted to help, but there was nothing I could do. So, I just hugged her back as hard as

I could. It surprised her, and I could feel her feel it. She gradually regained her composure and put me down.

"I'm so sorry, Clare... I really am," she said to my mother.

"Oh, Elsie, no. Don't ever be sorry for that. Never." My mother gave her a hug.

Looking back on it, I guess I represented the deepest longing in her heart, to have a child of her own. It had seemed so right, for so long, but she was reaching the sad conclusion that it just wasn't meant to be. Not for her.

That's always a major challenge in life. Something goes wrong, or one of your most cherished dreams doesn't come true, and deep disappointment sets in, darkening your vision. Ultimately, you just have to find your way past it. Elsie did, and ended up having a wonderful life.

"I hope I didn't..." she looked down at me as if she might have hurt me in some way.

"Who, him?" my mother asked. She looked at me with one of her loving smiles and stroked my cheek with the back of her hand. "Don't worry about him. He'll be fine."

***

About a year later, I was finally going to find out what my father did for a living. My mother was going to drop me off at his office for an hour while she went to an appointment in town. That's where he worked—"in town." She was going to the beauty parlor at John Wanamaker's, a giant department store across the street from his office. She would pick me up when she was finished.

She left me with the receptionist in the front lobby, who showed me into the anteroom of my father's corner office. His secretary sat at a large desk on one side of the room. A leather sofa and an armchair were on the other side, with a big glass coffee table in front of them. She told me that my father was wrapped up in a meeting and that I wouldn't be seeing him. But she had something important for me to do.

"Now, Davy," she said. "You know your daddy is an important lawyer, and he really needs your help today." That was news to me. I thought all I had to do was wait there until my mother came and got me. "You do know what a lawyer is, don't you?" she asked.

"Sure," I said. I still had no idea, but I didn't feel like letting her in on it.

A newspaper was lying on the coffee table. She looked at the front page for a few seconds. It had a big picture of an airplane on it. "Oh good," she said. "There it is." She sharpened a pencil and brought it over with a piece of tracing paper. She scotch-taped the tracing paper over the picture of the plane.

"Your daddy is in the middle of a very big case. He needs you to trace a picture of this plane so he can present it as evidence in the trial. He's going to use it in court." I looked at her, confused. "So, do a good job now, Davy. He needs this and he's really counting on you."

She went back to her desk and sat down. The phone rang, and she quietly took the call. I looked at the tracing paper taped over the picture of the airplane, then at the pencil with its freshly sharpened point. It reminded me of a needle at the doctor's office. Not a comforting sight for me.

"Oh my God, we're dead," I concluded to myself. "He's going to use a tracing of this plane for evidence, whatever that is. This is bad!"

I was never good at tracing, but I figured I'd better do my best and see if I could make it work. I tried as hard as I could, but the more I traced, the worse it got. Soon, it just looked like a piece of trash, but I kept going. I was pretty sure we were done for.

Then suddenly, my mother breezed into the room with her new hairdo, looking like everything was right with the world. She gave me a big smile, and I forced one back. I felt horrible. My father needed me, and I had let him down. My work was awful and the whole thing was a disaster.

She and the secretary launched into a quick chat about nail polish and lipstick. After a few minutes, my mother turned to me with a bright smile. "OK, come on, Duvy... we gotta go." She came over and grabbed me by the hand, but I didn't move.

"Wait, Mom. They need this for the court." I pointed at the tracing paper. My mother was baffled and looked over at the secretary, who got a big laugh out of it. She had probably forgotten about the whole thing. She came over and ripped off the tracing paper, crumpled it up, and threw it in the wastepaper basket.

"Oh! Don't worry about it." She chuckled. "I didn't get the chance to tell you, but we found out that we don't need it anymore. The judge called and said your dad won the case."

I was deeply relieved. That crap of mine would never have held up in court. And, I was pretty impressed with my father. He won the case on his own, without my evidence.

"Guess what I have waiting for you in the car?" my mother asked me, holding my hand as we walked toward the elevators. I had no idea. "Tastykake Krimpets!" she exclaimed. Suddenly, the world was made of pure butterscotch as the elevator doors opened. My mother swept me up in her arms, carried me in and gave me a big kiss on the neck. Ah, back to reality.

19

A Different Park

Things went along normally until June 1956, when suddenly the roof fell in. My parents gave us the terrible news: we were going to move. It was a death knell, and life as I knew it, was over.

We would be leaving our happy home in our beloved neighborhood and moving to a place called Melrose Park. I was devastated.

I had never heard of Melrose Park, but I knew a place called Burholme Park, and they were probably pretty much the same. Burholme Park was where we had our cousins-club picnic every spring. There were a few baseball diamonds there, along with some open fields. And as a municipal park, it had a bunch of one-room cabins scattered around that you could use for gatherings. Each cabin had a tiny sink and a windowless closet with a small, disgusting-looking toilet. You never wanted to go in there unless you really had to go.

It seemed like we'd be moving into one of these cabins, which was basically a shack. I didn't see how we were going to fit, but we'd have to make it work somehow. At least we'd still be together.

My father must have hit the skids with his law practice. I remembered that episode with the tracing paper and figured when you're running an operation like that, something like this was bound to happen sooner or later. Anyway, we had hit rock bottom and had to move.

Luckily, I was dead wrong. In fact, the exact opposite was true. The Philadelphia Warriors had won the 1956 NBA Championship. And although my father and Gotty never let anyone know their business, along with being General Counsel, my father probably had a piece of the team as well.

Whether or not that's where the money came from, he had made enough to move us out of the city into a new life in the suburbs. It was the 1950's American Dream come true.

Melrose Park was a stately suburb of Philadelphia, and my parents found a beautiful home there. Despite all my extreme paranoia about moving—and the word extreme is an extreme understatement—within just a few days of living there, I felt I had been transplanted into the kingdom of heaven.

We moved into a lovely Tudor-style home on a small street in a historic part of a place called Cheltenham Township. By today's standards, it was by no means a huge house; but back then, it was a small castle. As a gift to my parents, my grandfather hung wallpaper in every room.

It was full of charm and at least twice the size of where we'd lived before. But it was the grounds that really got me. We were in a world of nature that I hadn't known before.

As much as I loved the old neighborhood, it was largely a concrete realm. Our backyard was just the long driveway behind our house that separated us from the row of homes behind us. There were about twenty houses to a row on each side.

Now we lived on half an acre of verdant land, with a huge oak tree on the front lawn. And there was a beautiful flowering tree out back, with a small stream running next to it. Robins, cardinals, and blue jays serenaded us all day long.

Before, I was always playing with a ton of kids. But now, I spent a lot more time alone and was soon intoxicated by the natural sights, sounds, and smells that surrounded me. I made friends with some squirrels and rabbits that I saw every day, and I got to know a couple of turtles that lived in the stream. It was entrancing.

My mother blossomed there as well. She had grown up on a small farm in a rural part of New Jersey called South River, and now she was back in her real element. The place fit her like a glove and her hands were in the dirt all the time.

My brother, Michael, and I got a big room overlooking the front yard. Sybil got her own room next to us. Mike went to Cheltenham High School a few miles up the main street. Sybil and I went to Lynnewood Elementary, which had been built on some of the former back acres of Lynnewood Hall.

Mike and I always shared a room, which was great for me. He was eight years older, and I got countless benefits from it. He had become a teenager in 1954, just as rock 'n roll first came out. We had a record player and probably a hundred forty-fives that were on all the time. By coincidence, on the first Sunday night after we moved into our new home, Elvis Presley debuted on The Ed Sullivan Show.

Mike could do just about anything. He wired a stereo system in our new room, so he could play albums instead of just forty-fives. They called it a hi-fi back then.

My parents gave him a small area in the basement, which he converted it into his own darkroom. He got a high-end camera and would develop pictures down there.

Then, he got a reel-to-reel tape recorder and could work wonders with it, recording comedians like Steve Allen and Bob Newhart from the portable TV in our room. It might not seem like much now, but the technology was brand-new then, and it was miraculous.

As soon as he could drive a car, he started working under the hood and did a lot of his own maintenance. And every December, he would set up his intricate model train set in our basement. It had a whole town called Plasticville, USA, with a red-bricked Elementary School that was an exact replica of my new school. It was like a miniaturization of my life.

As his little brother, some of the things I picked up from him went on behind our parents' backs. Like, he'd call me into a room where he was hanging out with some friends and quiz me. "What's a four-letter word beginning with f and ending with k?" I'd shoot back the correct answer to everyone's delight and his obvious pride.

Sybil and I took a school bus to Lynnewood Elementary, and that bus ride spoke volumes about where we lived. Our house was across the street from a place called Latham Park, which was the only gated community in the area. Most of the wealthiest kids in the township lived there, and they all came to our bus stop.

At the very next stop, which was only one short block away, all the kids who lived in the small, quaint neighborhood called LaMott got on the bus. LaMott was a black community, and every black kid who went to Lynnewood lived there. So, we had quite a mix of kids on our bus.

Actually, the bus was voluntarily segregated, with one group of kids sitting in the front and another group sitting in the back. The girls sat in the front and the boys sat in the back.

It didn't take long for me to start loving those school bus rides. I had never been around any black kids before. Although they were a new cultural group for me, they were exactly the same as the other kids I had known all my life, and I soon got close with a bunch of them.

In reality, for elementary school boys in those days, all that really mattered was who was good at sports and who could be a bigger wiseass at the right time, which was basically all the time. I could hold my own in both, so it was all a lot of fun for me.

But there was also something subtle about our new neighborhood, a special atmosphere about it, almost like a nobility in the air. I couldn't quite put my finger on it, but intuitively, I felt a deep sense of respect for our surroundings.

Many years later, when I was researching a book on Abraham Lincoln, I learned that our little neighborhood had quite a history. It had been a critical location during the Civil War, and in a very real way, our bus stop was a distant reflection of it.

It had been built on the grounds that once belonged to Lucretia Mott, one of the fiercest abolitionists in American history. An ordained Quaker minister since 1820, she gave passionate speeches all over America and Europe against slavery, proclaiming it to be evil—an odious offense against God.

But she did more than just give speeches. She would never wear cotton or eat sugar because they were products of slave labor. And at serious personal risk, she used her home as a major stop on the Underground Railroad, sheltering a constant stream of runaway slaves who hid there on their way to freedom.

Then, during the Civil War, she made a bold move and allowed a large section of her land to be used as the encampment and training grounds for the first black regiment of the Union army. It was called Camp William Penn and was a national controversy. The Confederacy hated her for it.

After the war, her house was finally torn down, and Latham Park was built over the front part of the land. The ground behind it, where Camp William Penn had been, was turned into a small town of its own. Settled by waves of freed slaves coming north, they named it LaMott, in her honor.

So, our house had been built on her grounds, just a few hundred yards from where that noble drama had taken place. Who knows? Maybe the feeling I sensed was the atmosphere still ringing with the valor of those courageous souls.

In those days, Lincoln had urged his countrymen – "With malice toward none, with charity for all, with firmness in the right, as God give us to see the right, let us strive on to finish the work we are in..."

And they had done just that. Although we were separated by a hundred years of time, I felt proud of my old neighbors and was glad I had gotten to grow up on that ennobled ground.

20

Under Ashburn's Cap

As time went on, our lives seemed to prosper. My father's sphere of influence grew, and one thing I learned early as his son—he was always full of surprises.

Philly was a big baseball town and I was a serious fan. Even though the Phillies, our local team, seemed to have a permanent lease on last place, I didn't care. I followed every game and knew every player's batting average by heart.

We had one true legend: our center fielder, Richie Ashburn. He was more than a legend; he was an icon and is still one of the most beloved figures in Philadelphia sports history. Appropriately, he wore the number "1."

One night after dinner, my parents were getting ready to watch a show on TV. It was a play called "On Borrowed Time," something about a father who outwits death on behalf of his son. My father knew the lead actor from the old days in South Philly.

"Oh, here. I thought you might like this," he said and threw something at me that landed on the floor. I bent down to pick it up and to my absolute shock, it was a Phillies cap. Now, this was long before sports souvenirs were sold on every corner. You never saw one of these anywhere. Nobody had one and I couldn't believe it.

"Turn it over. Look at the brim," he said as the show started.

I did and saw a number "1" written in blue ink in the middle of the brim, right near the headband. It took me a second to realize what that meant, but when I did, I could hardly move. I was holding Richie Ashburn's cap.

I took it up to my room, put it on my bed and stared at it for a while. The enormity of what had happened began to sink in. With its deep-red color and super-rich texture, it was like a religious icon, a beatific holy relic. Sitting alone, in a state of reverence, I finally put it on. It fit my head perfectly, which, for some reason, I knew it would. I was transfixed, transformed, or whatever else you can imagine would be happening inside the mind of a ten-year-old boy who had just been granted a boon from baseball heaven.

I wore it to school for the next few days. During recess, all my friends came over to see it. I let them hold it, but I had made up my mind not to let anyone try it on. It didn't matter. Nobody even asked me. They were too much in awe.

***

One Sunday afternoon in September, my father had to go see my grandfather about something and invited me to come along with him. I grabbed my baseball glove and a tennis ball, so I could play on the front porch while they talked. Before we left, I put on Ashburn's cap.

We had a new 1959 Cadillac convertible, powder blue with a white canvas top. It was the style with the huge tail fins, and it only lasted that one year. He put the top down and we cruised over.

My grandfather was sitting outside, on the small porch in front of their house. My father sat down with him and they got right into their conversation, and I got right into throwing my ball against the steps. In no time flat, I was in the middle of an imaginary game of step-ball between two imaginary teams, announcing it in my head, like it was on radio.

At one point, I heard my grandfather's singsong voice. "Dave-a-la." I looked over at him and he stared at me with my Phillies cap, my baseball glove, and my tennis ball. I wore shorts, a Phillies T-shirt, and some black high-top Converse sneakers.

"What country are you from?" he asked me.

I had never been asked anything like that before and had no idea what he meant.

"What?" I asked him.

"What country are you from? You know. You're a citizen of what country?"

"I'm an American. I'm a citizen of the United States of America," I answered. His strange question didn't make any sense to me.

He looked me over once again. "I lived in a country once, and I thought I was from there, too—a citizen of that country." He paused. "And you know what happened?"

"Oh, come on, Pop," my father interrupted.

"No, no," Zayde said. "He's old enough now. He should know."

My father just shook his head but didn't say anything.

"You know what happened to me, Tot-a-la? One day, a soldier came up to our house with a rifle and pointed it at my father." He gestured like he was aiming a rifle at me. "And he said, 'OK, Jew, get out.' And we had to leave.

There was a Jewish community there for more than a hundred years and within a month, it was all gone." It sounded like a story from the dark ages, but I just looked back at him and didn't say anything. "Don't forget that," Zayde said. "It can happen to you."

I looked over at my father's new Cadillac, parked next to the curb. With its rocket fins, it looked like a spaceship. I glanced at my father, who was his usual calm, confident self. He always underplayed it, but when he was around, everyone always knew who had the real power in the room. Then I looked back at my grandfather.

"Hey Zayde," I thought to myself, "I'm wearing Ashburn's cap, and that kind of crap ain't gonna happen anymore."

Even though I didn't say it out loud, he looked like he heard it and gave me a halfhearted smile, probably at my youthful confidence, buoyed by its lack of experience.

"Nothing is for certain here," he said, finally. "Anything can happen to you in this life. Remember that."

He and my father shifted back into Yiddish. I straightened out Ashburn's cap, shook the whole thing off and got back into my step-ball game.

In that moment, the three generations on that porch covered a span of only sixty years. But they weren't just any sixty years. They were six decades of unprecedented, radical change. My grandfather was born before electricity and had to run for his life from the Old World. My father had been born between cultures and didn't even speak English until he went to school. And there I stood, the quintessential American kid, living in modern times, with the sixties about to begin in just a few months.

The differences between us were so vast, instead of being from another generation, I could have just as easily been from another planet.

The Story Begins

Clockwise from top left:

Wilt—
Following the trade to the 76ers,
shortly after his return to Philly
(SCRC – Temple University – Phila. PA)

Ike—
Founder & Co-Owner of
the 76ers— Publicity Photo
as General Manager
(SCRC – Temple University – Phila. PA)

Me—
Almost 16. Two weeks to the
day before Ike gave me the
news about the big trade.
(Courtesy Susan & Stan Needle)

High School Warrior

Above: 6'10" High School powerhouse – already drafted by the Philadelphia Warriors *(SCRC – Temple University – Phila. PA)*

Below, from left to right: Mock contract signing with Gotty at press conference *(SCRC – Temple University – Phila. PA)*; Wilt and Ike execute the real deal *(SCRC – Temple University – Phila. PA)*

The Big Dipper

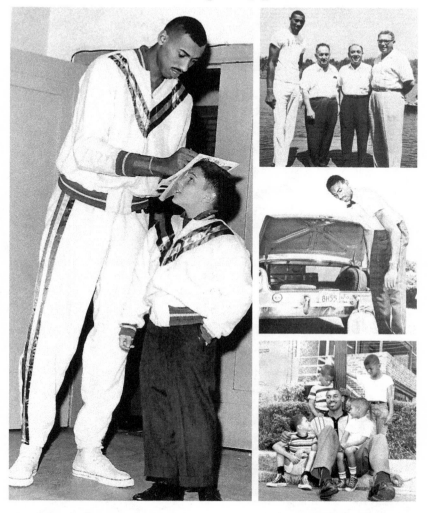

Left: Moments before a game. If you look at his head and the door, you'll understand the nickname, The Big Dipper.
(SCRC – Temple University – Phila. PA)

Right, top to bottom: The gang at the lake at Kutchers in the Catskills—Wilt, Gotty, Ike, Milt Kutcher. *(Courtesy Mark Kutcher)*; The greatest bellhop in the Catskills—Wilt working his job at Kutchers. *(Courtesy Mark Kutcher)*;and the young Warrior on the street with the kids. Wilt takes some time out to hang with the younger set.
(SCRC – Temple University – Phila. PA)

I follow tradition. Wilt shatters it.

Top: The summer before the big season. Wilt visits Camp Kweebec
(Courtesy Alan Witman)

Center, from left to right: Wilt reaches the peak – the most points ever scored in an NBA game – March 2, 1962. *(Associated Press)*; Eight days later, at my Bar-Mitzvah. (Quite a week for Ike!); My grandfather shows me the ropes.

Below: Our Family At the party – Sybil, Me, Clare, Ike, Merle, Mike

Forming the 76ers

Above: The Owners and their new star. Ike, Dolph Schayes, Koz
(SCRC – Temple University – Phila. PA)

Left: Naming the new team—Ike announcing the name - The Philadelphia Seventy-Sixers. I thought it was horrible. I had submitted the Philadelphia Spartans. He hated it. *(SCRC – Temple University – Phila. PA)*

Right: The new logo—Ike designed it at his cousin's ad studio. *(NBA Properties, Inc. © 2018)*

First Generation Americans

Top: Clare at age 8; Ike at age 13.

Center: The young lawyer—just starting out; Clare and Ike—happy newlyweds in 1938.

Bottom: On an international trip, touring Israel; A dance at Mike's wedding. The Great Zink looks on.

Way Back When, In '67

Clockwise from top left:

With the Championship in hand, Wilt executes a "Dipper Dunk" over Russ. *(SCRC – Temple University – Phila. PA)*; The Ball Belongs to Clare—Wilt arrives at the airport after the big win, championship ball in hand. It's for my mother. *(SCRC – Temple University – Phila. PA)*; A matter of reach—Wilt and Ali pose for the cameras. The size differential was vast, but the idea of a fight was mainly a PR stunt. *(SCRC – Temple University – Phila. PA)*; Young love—Sally and me, on our way to my Senior Prom.

A Legacy in Time

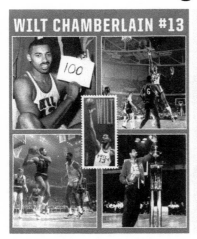

WILT CHAMBERLAIN #13

ANCIENT WARRIORS

*And other tales from the times when
Eddie Gottlieb was Mr. Basketball, men were men
and the two-hand set shot was king.*

The year was 1962. When the National Basketball Association began its season in October, there was, for the first time in the league's 16-year history, no professional basketball team in Philadelphia.

The Warriors, Eddie Gottlieb's boys, the team that won the very first league championship, had left town—gone to San Francisco. Philadelphia, a cornerstone franchise of the NBA, a big-league town that prided itself on its teams and its loyal, knowledgeable fans, was left with nothing but memories, bewilderment and faint hope.

It wasn't that Gottlieb stiffed the city, or that the fans turned on him. "Gotty" was a Philly guy, everyone knew that. Hell, he was a legend. People called him "The Mogul." The man had been promoting sports events in town for the past 40 years. Baseball, football, softball, wrestling—from neighborhood sandlots to downtown arenas, Gotty always had something going.

But it was basketball that Gottlieb loved best. He was born in 1898, only seven years after a janitor in a New England YMCA forgot to throw out two peach baskets, which were then nailed to the gymnasium wall by a young phys. ed. instructor named James Naismith, who was trying to invent what he called "an indoor sport out of a modified American rugby game." The first teams of what became basketball had

EYE ON THE BALL: Court-side kingpins Ike Richman and Eddie Gottlieb.

resented the South Philadelphia Hebrew Association. Coached by Gottlieb, the Sphas soon became a dominant force in professional basketball. Leagues, teams and players came and went rapidly in those

"For a stretch in the '30s," recalled the late Dave Zinkoff, a longtime Gottlieb friend and Sixers announcer, "one of Gotty's players, Gil Fitch, was the band leader at the Broadwood. Eddie would excuse him in the fourth quarter, and Fitch would

Clockwise from top left:
Wilt Postage Stamp—in December 2014, the Wilt Chamberlain Limited Edition Forever Stamp was released. Fifty million were printed. He is the only player to receive this honor. *(USPS)* ; Ancient Warriors—Philadelphia Magazine celebrates the golden days. *(Philadelphia Magazine)* ; The Ranger's End—my grandfather recording some prayers during his final days; Hall of Fame ceremony— the induction of Ike and Koz in 2008. Sybil Gabay, Don Richman, Ike Richman, Me, Sally, Evan Richman

21

The Big Dipper

Philadelphia's NBA team, the Warriors remained a central part of our lives. I had gotten old enough to understand the game and was completely involved with the team. And although my father was still the General Counsel, his role seemed to have expanded.

His relationship with Gotty, the team's owner, was closer than ever and the NBA season that was about to begin a few weeks later, in the fall of 1959, was going to be enormous for them. They had made a brilliant move a few years earlier that was about to pay off in a major way.

Gotty knew Philadelphia basketball like no one else, and he always kept his ear to the ground. At one point in the early 1950s, he heard about a remarkable ninth grader who was about to start Overbrook High School. The kid was over six-nine and could already dunk a basketball. His name was Wilt Chamberlain.

Gotty started paying close attention to him. By Wilt's sophomore year at Overbrook, he was six-eleven, weighed two hundred pounds, and was scoring thirty points a game. Tales of incredible strength and almost superhuman stamina were springing up everywhere. Over two hundred colleges got interested in him.

And so were most of the owners of the NBA. But Gotty and my father outmaneuvered them. With a few tweaks to the old territorial draft rule, they were able to secure the unquestionable rights to Wilt. They drafted him at the end of his junior year at Overbrook High.

He went to the University of Kansas. But after three years, a plan was hatched for him to leave college and play for the Harlem Globetrotters for a year. Then he would join the Warriors.

Nobody really knows exactly how the deal with the "Globies" got made, but the owner, Abe Saperstein, was part of an inner circle of basketball old-timers, who knew each other very well. They were old friends who were also rivals, or old rivals who were also friends. Whichever, they had their own way of working things out.

It was great for Wilt. He got paid an unheard-of amount of money—$65,000 for the year, along with a $10,000 signing bonus. At the time, the president of the United States was only making $20,000. And Abe got Wilt for a year, making every single "Trotters" game an automatic sellout.

It was great publicity for the Warriors and the NBA as well. Having Wilt touring the country with the Globies was much more beneficial to the league than having him play out his senior year in Kansas.

I never took the Globetrotters seriously because they didn't play a real game. It was more of a basketball show. Years later though, I was surprised when Wilt told me he felt the Globies were the greatest ballplayers in the game, far better than the NBA. He loved his season with them, playing all over the world.

The time finally came for him to join the Warriors, my father drew up the contract, and Wilt signed it with him at a ceremony for the press. They already had a deep relationship by then. My father was his personal attorney and financial advisor, as well as one of his most trusted friends. It was obvious they were on a wavelength all their own.

***

On October 24, 1959, Wilt appeared in a Warriors uniform for the first time and immediately transformed the game. It's hard to grasp how big a sensation he was, but there had never been anyone like him before. Taller and stronger than everyone else, he was also an extremely talented athlete, full of grace and coordination. On the court, he was virtually unstoppable. But he was also a new kind of black athlete and had a major impact on American culture as well. Along with his talent, he was confident and charismatic, with an irresistible layer of wit and charm. And he had a sharp mind, with a keen understanding of his value to the sport.

Back then, things changed very slowly in society. It had been less than a hundred years since the Civil War and the end of slavery. And it had been only twelve years since Jackie Robinson had broken the color barrier in Major League Baseball. Just three years earlier, when the Warriors won the NBA championship, there was only one black player on the team.

Suddenly, this superman came along and blew the doors wide open. Within a year, Wilt Chamberlain was the most recognized celebrity in the entire world. And he was also becoming a very wealthy young man. He was getting the highest salary in the history of sports, and my father was watching over every penny, making sure his funds were safe, secure and growing at a steady pace.

During the season, we always sat in our usual courtside seats, right under the basket. Gotty had a special warm-up jacket made for me. It was an exact replica of the team's uniform, and I wore it to every game.

One night, as they were about to go out on the floor, my father took me into a room near the court. Suddenly, Wilt popped in, and my father gave him a program and a pen. He put the program on top of my head and used it as a support to sign his autograph. A newspaper photographer snapped a quick picture and the next day, it was on the front page of the sports section of the Sunday paper. For me, it was a really big deal for a little while.

Wilt was named Rookie of the Year and MVP. He averaged 37 points and 27 rebounds a game. (They didn't keep records of blocked shots or assists back then, so there were no triple-doubles, like today. If they had, Wilt's records in those areas would have been off the charts.) The team had the third-best record in the league and won the Eastern Division semifinals. But the Boston Celtics beat us in the finals, four games to two.

The next year was almost an exact duplicate. Wilt averaged 38 points and 27 rebounds per game. We still had the third-best record in the league, but we got swept in the semifinals by the Syracuse Nationals, and we never even faced the Celtics, who went on to win the title once again.

***

But the NBA season that followed, 1961–1962, was one for the books. Some of the records Wilt set that year will probably never be broken.

For me, it all started early, during the summer of 1961, when Wilt made a surprise visit to my summer camp. I went to Camp Kweebec, which was owned by my parents' closest friends, Herman and Katherine Witman—always

Uncle Herman and Aunt Katherine to us. It was an idyllic place. My brother, sister, and I, along with two of our close cousins, went there forever.

The summer of 1961 was already my fifth year, and like all the other kids, I was a comic-book addict. I had been a major Superman fan and was amazed by the fact that on Krypton, his home planet, his name was Kal-El. That was the term I had learned from my grandfather that meant "vessel of God." It turned out that the two guys who had created Superman were Jewish and had chosen that name deliberately.

But this summer I had gotten introduced to a new company called Marvel Comics and it was expanding my imagination. They still featured action stories, but they dropped in some extra tidbits. In the last Fantastic Four, there was an alien named "The Watcher," from an advanced race of beings. He had become friends with Reed Richards, the Fantastic Four's leader.

One day, Richards wanders into The Watcher's laboratory when he isn't there and picks up a baton-like device. Suddenly he's rooted to the ground, can't move and his head begins to morph into a much larger size. The Watcher bursts in, grabs the baton out of Richards's hand and brings him back to his normal size.

Once Richards is fully restored, The Watcher explains that the device was a "consciousness enhancer" and in those few seconds, it had evolved him forward a thousand years, and he had become a human being of the distant future.

As a fellow scientist, he asks Richards what the experience was like. Richards says he couldn't retain the details, but he could remember that he had gone into a heightened state of awareness and was fully merged with the power of the universe. The joy of it was indescribable.

Now, I was always an impressionable kid. When I read Superman, I would daydream that I could fly and bend steel with my bare hands. I didn't know what to make of this new stuff, but I couldn't wait for the next episode.

Every Sunday morning at camp, we would go to buy comics at a stand that was set up in a grove of trees. On the first Sunday in August, as I was waiting in line, Wilt suddenly stepped out from behind a tree and surprised me. For a second, it didn't make any sense. Then, my father popped out from behind a different tree and I put two and two together.

They had come up for a special day at the camp. Wilt did an incredible basketball exhibition and then took pictures with each bunk. Everybody had a great time— except me.

For some reason, I really didn't like it when my parents came into my world, like visiting me at school or camp. I'm sure there's a good psychological explanation for it, but I found it unbelievably embarrassing. And as cool as it was that my father was visiting with Wilt, I couldn't wait for them to leave.

I got invited to eat lunch with them at the head table with Uncle Herman and Aunt Katherine. I don't remember how I did it, but I weaseled my out. I just wanted to be with my bunk.

It ended up being a great day and everyone came away with lifelong memories. Summer ended, and the next thing I knew, I was back in school, and the NBA season was about to begin.

***

In that incredible 1961-1962 NBA season, Wilt played on a level that had never been seen before and hasn't been seen since. He averaged 50.4 points a game and over 25 rebounds. Those are averages. And as amazing as those numbers are, there is one truly astounding statistic that really shows what he was made of.

When the season ended, which was eighty regular games and twelve playoffs—ninety-two games - Wilt had played every single minute of every single game. There was one twelve-minute stretch when he got ejected for arguing with the ref, but other than that, he never left the floor— never got injured, never got sick, and never took a break. He was on the court every single minute of every single game, the entire season.

And those weren't relaxed minutes either. Far from it. He was always the absolute center of attention, and all the action revolved around him. The other team hit him as hard as they could, double and triple-teaming him and playing as dirty as they could get away with.

On March 2, 1962, the Warriors had a game against the New York Knicks in Hershey, Pennsylvania. It was a school night, so neither my brother nor I could go. But we listened to the whole game on the radio.

That afternoon, my father had driven up to Hershey to spend a few hours with Wilt, who had gotten there early. He hadn't slept at all the night before and thought he was coming down with a cold.

To kill some time and calm his nerves, my father took him out to get something to eat and then over to a small amusement arcade that had a bunch of pinball machines and a shooting gallery.

According to Wilt, he seemed to be in a magic zone; no matter what he did, he couldn't miss. At the shooting gallery, he hit every single target, sometimes hardly aiming. He was on fire.

And that night during the game, as slightly sick

and tired as he was, whatever hot streak he was on went nuclear. He still could hardly miss and ended up scoring an undreamed-of 100 points.

It was a feat heard around the world and has stood the test of time. For more than half a century, Wilt has held the number one position in points scored per game. He holds 7 of the top 10 positions of points scored per game as well.

***

The season ended in one way that was predictable and in another way that wasn't. On the predictable side, the Celtics beat us in a bruising, heartbreaking seven-game series. On the unexpected side, after the season ended, the Warriors were sold to an investment group in San Francisco. My father had been secretly negotiating the deal for several months.

It was devastating news. For the first time since 1946, there would be no professional basketball team in Philadelphia. Wilt and the team were gone, creating a real void.

My father must have done well on the sale, though. Within a few months of it, we moved into a bigger, more modern home.

22

Fistfight?

Our new house was a beautiful, sprawling property on a corner lot, right near the old Widener estate. It marked a couple of new beginnings for me as I started eighth grade.

My parents had a suite on the first floor, and my sister and I had the whole second floor to ourselves. My brother, who had always been my roommate, had gotten married. He and his wife moved into an apartment about three miles away. So, I had my own room for the first time, and felt much more grown-up.

With the Warriors gone, our normal routine of following them and going to the games was over. But my father still stayed in close touch with Wilt. They continued their business relationship, and he was still one of my father's main clients.

I didn't know it—in fact, nobody did—but my father was secretly working on a deal to buy an NBA team and move it to Philly. He had started working on it even before he closed the Warriors sale.

He was trying to buy the Syracuse Nationals, who were our bitter rivals. Only the Celtics were more hated by our fans. He and their owner had agreed in principle on the sale. The purchase price was $700,000. My father had $350,000 of it. Now he had to find a partner to put up the other half.

First, he approached his closest childhood friend and one of his largest clients, Irv "Koz" Kosloff, who turned him down flat. Koz didn't want to get involved. He owned a profitable paper company and was focused on expanding it.

So, my father went out to the rest of his world of family and friends. To his amazement, nobody wanted to touch the deal. One of his cousins, who owned an ad agency, said, "Ike, professional sports have peaked. The next thing you know, you guys are going to be charging five bucks to go to a game. Who the hell is going to pay five dollars to go to a basketball game?"

He had a point. It was 1962, and a candy bar was a nickel, a bottle of Coke was a dime, and a gallon of gas was a quarter. And you could see a movie for fifty cents. My father was getting absolutely nowhere, so he kept badgering Koz, who kept saying no.

***

One Saturday morning, I was standing on the steps of Temple Sholom after services. My father was still inside, talking to a few men about some synagogue matters, all in Yiddish. The conversation had gotten a little heated and it looked like it was going to drag on, so I decided to wait outside.

As I was standing there, a taxicab made a sharp U-turn in the middle of the street and screeched to a halt next to the curb. When the cabbie jumped out, I realized it was my great-uncle, my father's Uncle Ike. (There were a lot of "Ikes" on my father's side of the family.)

Although they were extremely close, my father and his uncle couldn't have been more different. While my father's work world was a realm of refined, educated professionals, Uncle Ike was a denizen of the streets. He was a great guy, but still pretty rough around the edges.

"Hi, Duvid," he said, taking off his dark sunglasses and stuffing them into the pocket of his rust-brown leather jacket. "Where's your father?"

"Oh, he's inside fighting with Muttel Potash," I replied casually. Muttel was one of the older guys and was in charge of the bar mitzvah lessons.

"Fistfight?" Uncle Ike snapped back, on high alert. He unzipped his jacket and stepped toward the building, completely ready to rumble.

"No!" I responded immediately, stopping him. I almost burst out laughing, but I held it in. The idea that my father might be in a fistfight with somebody was the most absurd thing I'd ever heard. Not to mention in the synagogue, with an eighty-year-old man over bar mitzvah lessons!

"No, no, nothing like that," I assured him, smiling. "Just some shul stuff." That seemed to calm him down. He obviously had a short fuse and had been ready to go.

In another minute, my father came out of the front door and walked down the steps to meet us. The two of them talked to each other in Yiddish. From their tone, I could sense that Uncle Ike had come up with an idea, and my father, with all due respect, had given him a clear "Thanks, but no thanks." It was a quick interlude, and we left.

***

A few weeks later, I saw Uncle Ike again. My mother was thinking of adopting a dog, a big Afghan poodle that belonged to an old woman who couldn't care for it anymore. I was supposed to go take a look at the dog and see if it was too big for our house. "Isaac Ruvah will drive you over," she said. "He knows the old lady pretty well."

"Isaac Ruvah" was another name for Uncle Ike. When you talked to him directly, you always called him "Uncle Ike." But when you referred to him in the third person, he was Isaac Ruvah. Ruvah was a nickname. There were so many Isaacs, they gave each one a Yiddish modifier, so you could tell who they were talking about. It was like an Italian family that had so many Paulies, they had to give them nicknames like Paulie Walnuts, Paulie Bag o' Donuts, and so on. It was that kind of thing.

A few days later, Uncle Ike picked me up, and we drove over to the woman's apartment. He said her name was Cousin Agnes and asked me if I knew who she was. When I told him I didn't, he wasn't a bit surprised and explained that she was the widow of one of my father's cousins, Natey Schaeffer. He asked me if I knew who he was.

"I'm sure you don't," he said before I even had a chance to answer. And he was right. I had never heard of him, but that was nothing new. Our extended family was huge and a lot of them didn't speak English, so to me, they were a big blur.

Uncle Ike didn't say anything for a few moments as he drove. His salt-and-pepper hair, now far more salt than pepper, shimmered in the flickering sunlight as it poured through the windshield. Then, with a smile of both irony and affection, he started telling me about this unfamiliar relative, and I quickly understood why I had never heard of him before.

Apparently, Cousin Natey was a Jewish gangster, and a fairly significant one at that. As with most American subcultures, the Jews had a dark side, a criminal underbelly. And like the Irish, the Italians, the African-Americans, the Asians, and so on—they didn't like to talk about it. To them, it was best kept private. Natey had been dead for quite some time, but it was clear that Uncle Ike's memories of him were still very much alive.

"Yeah, Cousin Natey was really something. There was never anybody like him," he mused. "He was our cousin, a first cousin to your Bubbe and me, and we were really close."

He got quiet again, like he was trying to decide how much of the vault he wanted to open. "Listen, this is just between you and me, so don't talk about it to anybody, but he was with Meyer Lansky."

He looked at me like he had just revealed a great truth, but I had never heard that name before. As it turned out, Meyer Lansky was the most notorious alleged Jewish mobster in American history, but it meant nothing to me.

Since he sounded important, I figured he might have owned one of the stores on Castor Avenue, the neighborhood's big shopping strip. I knew it couldn't have been the toy store because the brothers who owned it, Hershel and Zvi Slansky, were tight with my parents. But there were dozens of others.

"You know who that is, don't you?" he asked.

"Sure!" I shot back.

"OK, good. So, during prohibition, Natey and his group ran Philly for Lansky," he said. "Made a fortune."

"A lot of people in the family were ashamed of him, but not your Bubbe," he went on. "No sir. She would never let anyone say anything bad about him. She wouldn't hear of it. And I'll tell you one thing, you don't ever want to get on her bad side."

As tough as he was, Uncle Ike was my grandmother's baby brother, the youngest of eight, and I could hear a definite sound of intimidation in his voice. It was surprising because to me, she was just my sweet grandmother. She was always full of love, and although I could barely understand her, I always felt it. She'd lived here longer than fifty years and still sounded like she just got off the boat. It didn't matter though. Her hugs and kisses, and the light in her eyes told us everything we needed to know. She was all heart, and Uncle Ike's comment about her fierce loyalty made perfect sense.

"If somebody had a bar mitzvah or a wedding and they couldn't afford it, Natey would always cover it," Uncle Ike continued. "Same thing with a shiva. If somebody in the family died and they didn't have the money, Natey was right there. Great guy!"

A shiva is a gathering that happens at a mourner's house, and there's always a lot of food put out for the visitors. Before then, it hadn't occurred to me that you had to pay for it. Somehow it seemed to come along with the death.

"Cousin Agnes is really something," Uncle Ike said as we got to her apartment. When we walked up to the door, he took out his own key.

"She was a flapper, you know? Great dancer. I don't know how they met, but she was a real looker and Natey fell hard for her."

He opened the door, bent down, and picked up the mail. "She was a real shiksa [a non-Jewish woman] too. That was another big strike against him with the family. But Natey didn't give a shit. He was nuts for her. My God, she was pretty, though. Really, really gorgeous."

We walked down the hall, into a dimly lit bedroom

full of stale cigarette smoke. A huge white dog was lying at the foot of a double bed. And an unbelievably old, white-haired lady was lying in it. She looked like a creature in a comedy/ horror film, a kindly old ghoul who had been dead for years but could still smoke cigarettes. There was a bottle of clear liquid on her end table with a half-filled glass next to it. A pungent odor filled the air that I would later come to know as vodka.

Next to the bottle was a black and white picture in an ornate silver frame. Clearly from the Jazz Age, a dapper-looking guy in a sharp tuxedo was standing next to a curvaceous flapper in a short dress. She wore one of those 1920s hats that covered her forehead, framing her face with a perfect blend of pearls and curls. They were obviously at a fashionable party or some fancy joint, having an amazing time, and she had a dazzling smile.

"There's your Cousin Natey," Uncle Ike said, pointing to the picture. "And Duvid, take a guess who's on his arm." I shrugged. I didn't know, and I really didn't care. The whole scene was starting to get to me; I just wanted to get out of there. "That's right," he said, smiling at the pale ghost in the bed. "It's Agnes."

She lit another cigarette, took a long drag, and blew out an enormous billow of smoke. It didn't seem possible for that much exhaust to come pouring out of a body that small and frail. She gave me a wide smile. Her white skin crinkled into a thousand pieces, and her mouth revealed a smattering of teeth that were more orange than yellow.

"Boy, was she something," he mused, with a faraway look in his eyes. He peered into the dense cigarette smoke, like he was looking through a gray veil, at a dim vision of the distant past.

"You were one pretty lady, Agnes," Uncle Ike said

to her. "And according to Natey, nobody could do the Charleston like you. He always said there was magic in those hips of yours." He did some ridiculous Charleston imitation, swiveling his hips around like he was twirling a hula hoop, which really cracked her up. She laughed for a moment, then broke out into a long, hacking cough. She reached over, grabbed a tissue, and spit into it.

That did it. I really had to go. She seemed like a nice enough lady, but I couldn't handle being there any longer. I had never been around anybody that old before, and I wasn't prepared for it. I mean, Uncle Ike was up there in years, but next to her, he looked like a teenager. It was all just too much.

After another few minutes, we left. As far as I was concerned, I wasn't coming back. My mother could handle anything further with the dog. I was done.

Later that night, as I was lying in my bed, I was too agitated to fall asleep. We all know getting old is a fact of life, but this face-to-face encounter with it had really thrown me. In my mind's eye, I kept seeing that great old picture of Agnes and Natey. They were at the high point of their lives, young, happy and clearly in love. But the suave and handsome Natey was long since dead. And his vivacious showgirl had turned into this withered, ancient woman, confined to bed, lying in a shroud of smoke.

"Is this what's going to happen to me?" I wondered. But I knew the answer before I even finished asking the question. "Of course, this is what's going to happen to you," I replied to myself. "This is exactly what's going to happen to you. That is if you live long enough."

Images of the young Agnes and the old Agnes kept alternating in my mind, like someone was running a slideshow in there. It was hard to believe they were the same person.

"What else do you think is going to happen?" my inner dialogue continued. "How do you think this whole thing ends? One way or another, you die." After about an hour more of this mental back and forth, I finally drifted off. But I didn't sleep well that night.

***

We ended up getting the dog, and I soon forgot about the whole thing. But many years later, toward the end of her life, my mother told me the real story behind Uncle Ike's visit to my father on the synagogue steps that Saturday.

Apparently, the word had been out that my father was looking around for some money to close the Syracuse deal, and Uncle Ike thought he might be able to help. He still knew a few of Cousin Natey's associates and thought they might put it up.

My father quickly, politely, and very firmly declined. Instead, he continued on his path down the straight and narrow, searching for a partner. And he continued to come up blank.

Finally, after months of bending Koz's ear and his arm, his longtime childhood pal threw in the towel and decided to go in with him. Koz always said that in the end, he never could say no to Ike.

Within a month, the deal was done. The NBA Board of Governors approved it, and my father held a press conference. Beginning with the 1963–1964 season, the Syracuse Nationals would become Philadelphia's new NBA team.

23

Schayes for Two

My father became the General Manager and took charge of the team. Koz stayed largely in the background, focusing on his paper company. To me, it seemed ideal. Koz and his wife, Libby, were two of my parents' closest friends, and our families were always together. I can't remember a time without them.

They had a son who was about the same age as my brother and a daughter who was the same age as my sister. Whenever our families got together, the wives would go off together, the older sons would go off together, and the daughters would go off together. That left the two men to take care of the little boy, me. So, the three of us were thrown in together a lot.

It was perfect for them. I was young enough that I didn't know or care what they were talking about, and I was easily occupied. If we were indoors, any game or puzzle would do. And if we went out, all they had to do was bring a ball, like they were walking a frisky puppy.

Koz had a ton of money and was always buying me things. He was by far the richest person we knew, so I was surprised when I learned that he had grown up impoverished. He came from one of the poorest families in the neighborhood; they had absolutely nothing. Then, with no training or connections of any kind, Koz made all the money himself.

During the early days of the Great Depression, he started a one-man paper company. To be optimistic, he named it after the new US president, and Roosevelt Paper was born. At a relatively young age, Koz became quite wealthy. But to his dying day, he lived a somewhat modest lifestyle, never forgetting where he came from or what it took for him to get where he got.

My father had been his attorney ever since he'd finished law school, and Koz trusted him completely. Still, buying the Syracuse team was a risky move and Koz went in with a deep breath, as well as a deep sigh.

The first thing that had to happen was that the team needed a new name. My father came up with the idea of holding a "Name the Team" contest to try to get fans involved.

They got about a thousand entries and he finally selected The Philadelphia 76ers, which I thought was the worst name I'd ever heard. I hated it and couldn't believe he picked it.

But he knew what he was doing. He had to re-brand the Syracuse team, so he wanted a name that would be specific only to Philadelphia. As the birthplace of the nation, the home of the Declaration of Independence and the Liberty Bell, the name fit the bill perfectly.

He also knew it was going to be a tough job. But there's no way he could have known how tough. The first disaster was that President Kennedy was assassinated right after the second game of the season, making it a depressing time to drum up enthusiasm for a new sports team.

And on top of that, it was clear from the start that the city just wasn't behind them. They were the same group of guys we used to hate, just wearing Philly uniforms. And they were losing a lot of games. Attendance was dismal, never pulling more than two thousand people into the ten-thousand-seat arena. And most of those tickets were giveaways.

Then, to make matters worse, for some reason that's still unknown, a news blackout was imposed on the team by the powerful media company that owned two of the city's three newspapers. They instituted a policy that was a death sentence. If we lost, we'd get four paragraphs on the third page of the sports section; if we won, we'd get two paragraphs on the fourth page. It was brutal.

My father struggled through it bravely, though. He and Koz were prepared to lose some serious money in the beginning, and they did.

One of the only bright spots in those early days was his relationship with the star of the team, Adolph "Dolph" Schayes. At six-seven, he was one of the leading scorers and rebounders in the league, as well as a twelve-time NBA all-star. And he happened to be a Jewish ballplayer, which had become extremely rare. He was also one of the nicest guys in the world.

He and my father hit it off immediately, and my father took him under his wing. Dolph was heading toward the end of his career, so my father named him player/coach.

Late one afternoon, he brought him to our house for dinner. There was a long driveway on the side of our house. My father had installed a basketball hoop and backboard on a metal pole at the far end of it, near the garage. It was a great little court, and it became my world.

I was out shooting around by myself when my

father pulled up with Dolph in the car. They said a quick hello, and walked over to the back door, which was about fifty feet away from the basket.

"Dave!" Dolph shouted over to me, holding up both hands, signaling that I should throw him the ball. He was so far away that it took all my might to reach him. He caught the ball and assumed a perfect stance, taking aim at the basket. He was an acknowledged master of the two-handed set shot, which had dominated the game before the jump shot came along, but was rarely used anymore.

As soon as he took his stance, I knew something special was about to happen, and after a moment, he let it fly. From the time the ball left his hands, it was one of the most beautiful things I'd ever seen. The rotating sphere looked like a small brown planet as it arched its way across the sky. It seemed to hover in mid-air, high above the basket for a moment. Then, it fell straight down, plunging through the metal hoop without touching the rim—a perfect swish. And it popped the net in a way I had never seen or heard before.

Whenever you get the chance to see a true master's magic, there's nothing like it. It takes you to a new level of appreciation and something within you gets inspired. It stays with you, and in a subtle way, you're never the same again. He had just thrown in an incredible half-court set shot and the three of us stood there for a few seconds, soaking in the perfection of the moment. Then, they went inside.

During dinner, we had a great time. Dolph's Yiddish was excellent, and he and my parents chatted away in their private world. There was a lot of laughter and it sounded like they were trading a bunch of jokes. Yiddish humor is loaded with things the adults don't want the kids to hear, but I didn't care. I had grown up with it all my life. He stayed long past dessert.

The season continued on, but unfortunately, the team kept floundering. By the end, the papers were full of stories about what a dull beginning it had been and what bad shape we were in. Rumors were flying that my father had been talking to potential buyers, or that he was just going to close-up shop and quit. None of them were true.

The next year, 1964–1965, he made some improvements with the team. He had traveled to the Japan Olympics that summer to sign Luke Jackson, his first-round draft pick. It gave us some hope and a little spark, but we were still a drab team. We kept losing and the enormous Philadelphia fan base that was so critical to our success, didn't want to have anything to do with us.

Things kept going nowhere, until that magic night in January 1965, when my father changed everything. Suddenly the giant center for the 76ers wore the number 13, with the name "Chamberlain" written above it, and we were in a whole different world.

The lackluster season was quickly transformed into a high-speed rocket race for the title. We went at it full blast and almost made it, until that mid-April night, when we smashed headlong into a brick wall in the Boston Garden.

24

Keep the Hundred

Now, that it was the end of May, my cares about the 76ers faded into the background until next season. Tenth grade was almost finished, and summer was on the horizon.

For the first time in years, I wouldn't be going back to overnight camp. Instead, I'd be living at our house down the shore. It was my mother's idea. I had turned sixteen and could drive a car now, and she thought some new experiences might help me grow up. If I went back to camp, it would be more of the same, but down the shore, anything could happen.

About a week before I was ready to leave, my father invited me to come in town and see him at his office. Then we'd go out to dinner and a Phillies game.

As always, he was extremely busy. He had just merged his law firm, enlarging its client base. His younger partner, Don Jamieson, became the President Judge of the Philadelphia Court System. And Marvin Comisky, a close friend and associate, became Chancellor of the Bar. My father's considerable prominence in the legal community continued to expand.

And he was working on the team as well, with his eye on the championship, as always. He had become focused on a Baltimore Bullets guard named Wally Jones, who was a graduate of Overbrook High and also of Villanova University. He was a real local favorite but had recently run into some legal problems and dropped out of sight. Nobody knew where he was. My father put out some feelers to see if he could find him. He'd be perfect for the 76ers.

On the day of our appointment, I took the subway down to City Hall and walked the half block over to his building. It was only the second time in my life that I had been to his office. The first one was almost ten years earlier, with that airplane tracing fiasco.

When I got there, I walked into the very same waiting room, and the very same secretary greeted me. She was pretty much the way I remembered her, except it was ten years later, and we were both down the road a bit. I sat down on the leather couch and read the paper for a while. Then my father buzzed her, and she led me into his office.

When I first walked in, I was surprised at how big it was. On one side of the room, there was a small sitting area with a round conference table and four chairs. On the other side was my father, sitting behind a large, beautifully carved wooden desk. There was chair right next to it and a sofa against the side wall. Through the picture window behind him, I could see the statue of William Penn that stood on the top of City Hall. He was carrying a briefcase, just like a lawyer.

"Sit down," my father said, pointing to the chair next to his desk. I did and took a long look at him. I had never seen him at work before.

Everything about his appearance was perfect. His dark-brown suit was pressed. His white shirt was crisply ironed, and he wore a matching brown tie with a pattern of

160

the Lions of Judah on it. The State of Israel had given it to him in recognition for his service with Israeli Bonds, and he wore it often. I was a big Robin Hood fan and, to me, it always made him look like Richard the Lionhearted.

As I took him in, it hit me that although it was late in the afternoon, in the middle of the week on a workday, he looked like he hadn't done a thing. Not one hair was out of place. And on top of that, his glass-covered desk had absolutely nothing on it—not a folder, not a scratch pad, not even a piece of paper. Instead of looking like he worked there, he looked more like a model in a photo shoot.

"What do you really do here?" I finally asked him.

"What do you mean? You know what I do here. This is my office. I work here."

"Yeah, but there's nothing here. Where's all your stuff? You know, your work—like papers and folders. Stuff like that."

"Oh that. That's all put away," he said. "A place for everything, and everything in its place. But believe me, a lot gets done in here. Don't be fooled. You see those law books over there?" He pointed to a few books on a shelf. "Go over and take a look at them."

I went to the small bookshelf and scanned the titles.

"Those books are critical, some of my most important tools. And when you finish law school, I'm gonna give you the whole shelf. Believe me, it will definitely help you pass the bar," he said. "Push that one book on the right side."

I did, and the shelf automatically revolved around, turning into a small bar with a few liquor bottles and glasses on it. The books were just a flat façade.

"See what I mean?" he asked, seriously.

"Very funny," I said.

It was the kind of thing he did all the time. He was a real "kibitzer," which is Yiddish for someone who takes life with a grain of salt, along with a generous helping of humor. His friends always said he could have been a comedian.

But the gag bar was just that—a gag. Liquor had no part in his life. I had never seen him have a drink anywhere, at any time. It was the same thing with my mother. They weren't drinkers. But they were both heavy smokers. She was over a pack a day, and he always had a lit cigar going, usually one of the big ones.

He glanced down at his watch and looked up with a smile and said, "OK. Let's go have some fun!" We walked over to a famous steakhouse near his office and had a great dinner. Then, we took a cab over to the ballpark. Ernie Banks and the Chicago Cubs were in town.

We walked into the Phillies office, and an usher escorted us to our seats. Just being in the ballpark for a game at night was always mind-blowing. The enormous field lights had literally turned nighttime into day. It was seven-thirty in the evening and it could have been one o'clock in the afternoon.

Connie Mack Stadium was an archaic, old-fashioned baseball venue that opened in 1909. It could seat only about twenty-five thousand, and everything was extremely compressed. Back then the fans were much closer to the game than they are today.

I had no idea where our seats were, but as we walked along, they kept getting better and better. Finally, we got to the deluxe boxes, which were literally on the field itself. Our box was on the third base line, between the coach and home plate.

I couldn't believe it. I had never been that close before. I wasn't just watching the game, I was in it. I could see the expressions on the players' faces and hear them talk to each other. All the rest of the sounds of the game were unbelievably crisp as well. The sharp crack of the wooden bat as it hit the ball, the zing of the ball as it whizzed through the air, and the crisp smack it made in a player's leather glove when he caught it, all put me right in the action. And I could smell the grass, like they were playing in our yard. In short, I was in an ecstatic baseball trance.

Around the third inning, Bob Carpenter, the owner of the Phillies, came over and joined us along with his guest, Ford Frick, the commissioner of Major League Baseball, who happened to be in town. My father and I were sitting in the first row and after the introductions, he got up and sat with them, a few rows back. Of course, I didn't move. I was too enthralled and couldn't have cared less who they were.

The Phillies were having our usual lousy season, but as always, I still followed them religiously. Amazingly, though, we were having a great game. We went on to beat the Cubs, 6–0. They were having an even worse year than we were.

After the game ended, we took a cab home. As we walked up the driveway to the back door, my father put his arm around my shoulder. We stopped in front of the rose garden that my mother had planted outside the kitchen window, with its sea of red, yellow, white, and orange flowers. When you stood at the sink and looked out, all you saw was her bed of roses.

"They came in pretty good this year," he said as we stood there. He didn't say anything for a moment. "Do you know what I paid for tonight?" I didn't respond. I knew he was going into his teacher-mentor mode, which was something he did with me all the time. But I was a typical sixteen-year-old and already knew everything, so I only half-listened.

"All I paid for were the cab rides," he said. "That's it. Not the steak dinner. Not the box at the ball game. None of that. Just the cabs." It was a beautiful night, the world was approaching full bloom and the warm June air was soaked with dense, rich fragrances.

"And do you know why I didn't have to pay for any of it?" he continued. "Because it was all a gift. The owner of the restaurant is a client and a friend. The owner of the Phillies is a professional associate and a friend. And they were happy to do it. In fact, they would have been insulted if I had offered to pay."

We got to the back door and before we walked into the kitchen, he turned and said, "This is what happens when you get to a certain level, Duv. Everything changes, and they line up to do you favors. Remember that. When you are in the right place, at the right time, doing the right thing, it all works the way it's supposed to."

Many years later, when my mother was sick and approaching the end of her life, we were reminiscing about the old days, and I told her about that night and what my father had said to me.

"He left out one important thing," she said, smiling with her memories. "With Daddy, they all did him favors because of how much he had already done for them. Most of the time, people were just trying to pay him back. They were really just saying thank you."

***

A few days later, I was doing what I always did at the end of the day: endlessly shooting baskets in the backyard by myself. It was about five-thirty, and my father turned into the driveway, returning from work, as usual.

He always parked the car in front of the garage,

leaving the court open for me. But this time, he pulled all the way up and parked right under the basket. He turned the car off and motioned for me to get in. He had a serious look on his face. He had never done this before and something seemed wrong. I got in the passenger's side and sat down.

"Listen to me," he said soberly. "I've been giving this a lot of thought, and I've decided that you're old enough now to start doing some chores around the house. Your life shouldn't be all play, all the time. It's time you should start to get a little serious."

"OK," I said. This was something new, and I had no idea what to make out of it.

"Now, I thought we'd start out with the car," he said. He leased a new one every two years and had just gotten a Cadillac a few weeks earlier.

"So, here's what I want you to do," he continued. "If I have gotten the car washed, and it happens to rain on the same day that I got it washed, then when I get home, I want you to take a rag and wipe it down for me. It's no big deal. Just wipe the water off so that it doesn't bead up. It's a new car and I want to keep it nice."

"Sure," I said. "No problem."

"What a weird idea," I thought. "I'm only supposed to do this if he gets the car washed and it rains on that same day. What are the odds of that?"

"Now, I am willing to pay you for this," he began again. "I think it's only fair. And since we're starting a new arrangement between us, I'm willing to pay you in advance. I usually do that when I hire somebody new. It's a good idea." He reached over and slipped something into my hand. "Here."

I could tell it was a folded, crisp bill. I figured it was

a buck or maybe even a five, which would have been nice because that's what I got for my allowance every week. And it was plenty, easily covering all my expenses—school lunches, bowling, movies, everything. And I usually had money left over. So far, at the end of the school year, I had almost fifteen dollars saved up in my piggy bank.

He casually pulled out a cigar and lit it. As he did, I glanced down at the bill and saw the number "100" in the corner.

I couldn't believe my eyes. I had never seen a hundred-dollar bill before. I didn't even know they existed. Fives were common. You'd see a ten sometimes, and every once in a while, you'd run into a twenty. But never this.

I didn't know what to say. He was giving me twenty weeks' worth of allowance for this idea of his, which was ridiculous on the face of it. I appreciated his generosity, but in my mind, it was just too much.

"Look, Dad," I said. "We both know that I'm not going to do this car thing. You're not going to get the car washed and then it's gonna rain on the same day. And even if it does, I'm sure we're both gonna forget about it. This chore thing is never gonna happen."

He took a few puffs of his cigar and gazed contentedly through the windshield at our idyllic backyard, lush with flowers and vegetables, all carefully planted and nurtured by the farm girl he'd married, who was still the love of his life.

"Yeah, you're probably right," he said. "But you know what? Keep it anyway."

"Dad, don't you think this is a little extreme?" I responded. "Don't you think you might be spoiling me?" I really meant what I said, but to him, it was music to his ears.

"As long as that's the way you're thinking, I have absolutely nothing to worry about," he said firmly and smiled. Then he put his hand on my knee and shook it. "Don't worry about it, Duvid, you're not spoiled. You're coming along just fine. Keep the hundred."

We both got out of the car and started walking past the rose garden toward the back door. "Have fun this summer," he added with a smile.

25

A Royal Ride

A few days later, we moved down the shore, to our home in Longport, New Jersey. It was a lot of extra work for my mother, but she always loved it down there. In Elkins Park, she got regular help from her stalwart companion, Geneva. But in Longport, she was on her own, and things could get pretty insane. Sometimes, she would make lunch and dinner for up to sixteen people, often serving meals in two shifts.

But that never slowed her down. She had flower gardens with roses, tulips, and peonies out front, and a vegetable garden in the back with tomatoes, cucumbers, and peppers.

In the living room, she kept two small metal plaques on the mantelpiece over the fireplace that summed things up. One read, "The opinions expressed by the husband of this household are not necessarily those of the management." And the other—"Women's faults are many. Men have only two. Everything they say. And everything they do." And this was years before women's lib.

The summer started off well. I got a job at a day camp and it was much more fun than I thought it would be.

I made some new friends and settled into a nice routine.

One day, a co-worker offered to fix me up with his cousin for a blind date. He thought I'd like her, but he said she was pretty young. She had only just turned fifteen. Now I was almost sixteen and a half, and she was basically a fourteen-year-old, so I turned him down. But he kept working on it, insisting she was very mature for her age. I finally decided to give it a shot.

When I met her, I was surprised. To me, she could have easily been seventeen. She was nice, but it was kind of a bland blind date. We went to a movie, got some ice cream, talked some, and that was it.

About a week later, I decided to ask her out again. I called, and she readily accepted. I asked her what she wanted to do, and she told me just to come over and we'd figure it out when I got there.

"So, what do you want to do tonight?" I asked when I picked her up.

"I don't know," she answered. "What do you want to do tonight?" I thought I heard a coy tone in her voice.

"I don't care," I said. "Whatever you want."

"OK, great," she answered. "Let's go somewhere and park."

"OK," I said. I didn't want to show it, but I had absolutely no idea what she meant. I had never heard the word park used before, other than to just park your car. But as I was about to find out, it had a whole different meaning.

We drove around and found a dark, deserted street near the beach. She got out of the car and hopped into the back seat. I did the same.

For a moment, she stared out the window at the moon that had just risen over the ocean. As I looked at her in the moonlight, she had a young, sweet face, but the rest of her was like a Playboy centerfold with her clothes on. Her body was perfect, and her jeans were so tight, they seemed sewn on.

She looked at me with a funny expression, like she was about to tell me a secret and was sure I was going to like it. "I love sex," she said, matter-of-factly.

Of course, I found the news to be interesting, but there was something about the way she said it that didn't quite fit. From her everyday tone, she could have just as easily told me she really loved pizza. I wasn't quite sure if I'd heard her right.

But then, she reached up, stroked my hair with her long, perfect nails, and looked me in the eyes. After a moment, with a soft siren sigh, she said she found me incredibly attractive.

Was this real or was I dreaming? For a nice Jewish boy—a good student who always obeyed his parents and teachers, for that kind of kid—to hear this kind of news, coming from this kind of creature, under these circumstances, I had to think, "Hey, you know what? Maybe there really is a God after all."

In another moment, she was ready to turn words into deeds, and with the car windows fogging up, she got the ball rolling. I was a late bloomer, and not very experienced. She was from a different part of town, where they obviously ran on a much faster track. And it was immediately apparent that she was a thoroughbred, who really knew how to move.

I didn't know what hit me. Two hours went by in a flash and by the end of it, I felt like I'd been run over by a Mack truck. Within days, we were in a serious relationship.

Now, to use the old baseball metaphor, before then, I had only gotten to first base a couple of times, but always on walks, never on hits. Suddenly, I was starring in the majors, hitting stand-up doubles and triples off the wall in every game, to the delight of the delirious crowd.

It was like my starving hormones had been given a free pass to a nightly, all you can eat buffet. The place had everything and the more I ate, the hungrier I got. Before I knew it, a month and a half had been burned up in the sizzling summer heat.

***

One afternoon in mid-August, when I came home from camp, I saw a really unusual car parked in front of our house. I knew every make and model by sight, but I had never seen anything like this thing before. I was about to find out it was something called a Bentley.

I walked into the house, and there was Wilt, sitting at our dining-room table having a cup of coffee with my mother. We were really glad to see each other again. I hadn't seen him since the Celtics disaster.

"Hey, Big Guy," he said, flashing me one of his megawatt smiles. "How you doin'?"

"Great," I said and went over and shook his hand, which was always an awkward experience. His hands were triple the average size, and there was no way you could have a regular handshake with him.

We talked for a while. He had just come back from the west coast and had taken an apartment in town. Training camp was only a couple of weeks away, and it was time to start getting ready for the season. My father and Gotty were driving down from Philly together and would be there in time for dinner.

He shifted into telling me all about his car and asked if I wanted to take a ride with him. We walked outside and looked it over.

The Bentley is a super-high-end British luxury car, even more exclusive than a Rolls-Royce. Apparently, it's what the royal family rides around in. This one had been custom-made for Wilt, with an oversized driver's seat that was specially positioned more to the rear, for extra leg-room.

"I'd let you drive it, but there's no way you could," he said. "Here, try it." He opened the driver's door. I sat on the huge seat and my feet didn't even make it halfway to the pedal. We both laughed. I got out and walked around to the passenger's side. He got behind the wheel and we pulled away.

It was the first time I ever saw him in an environment that really suited him, and I loved it. He was able to be relaxed and free in there, not cramped up in some miniature space made for average-size people. Some years later, I felt the same way when I visited him in the mansion he had built for himself in Bel Air.

We started driving around and making some small talk. Then, out of nowhere, he asked—"Who is she?"

"Huh?" I responded casually. His direct question had taken me by surprise and I held my cards close to the vest.

"The chick," he answered. "You know, the girl you're into. Who is she?" I didn't respond.

"Come on, you know what I'm talking about. What's she like? I hear she's really nice."

I told him a very little bit about what was going on, just a few minor details, then I asked, "How do you know about her, anyway?"

"I read about it in the LA Times," he said sarcastically.

"No, really."

"No, really. You're big in LA," he replied dryly.

A few seconds went by. "How do you think I know about her?" he finally asked. "Your dad told me."

That was a huge surprise. I had discussed the situation briefly with him only once, in the very beginning. I had told him that I was going out with somebody. He asked me what her father did for a living. I told him he was a doctor and he said, "Nice." That was it.

I never talked about her with anyone other than a few friends, not even my brother, and certainly never my mother. I couldn't believe my father even remembered our conversation from way back then.

"What are you, surprised, man?" Wilt asked me.

"Yeah," I said. "I guess. I mean, I didn't know he knew all that much about it."

"Oh, come on, David," he said, like he was talking to a first grader. "Your father knows every single thing about you. He always knows where you are and what you're up to. You can take it from me, he knows everything you're doing, all the time."

Then, turning on a dime, he started grilling me on how much I knew about getting girls pregnant—or more specifically, about not getting girls pregnant. Once he had a feel for my knowledge of the subject, he went into a detailed lecture about the ins and outs of the whole thing. Not surprisingly, he was an expert. After all, entrapment in a paternity suit is a major occupational hazard in his line of work.

The ride seemed to go on forever, and I was really glad when we finally got home. It had been kind of cool, but still pretty awkward. I was relieved when we went into the house and things got back to normal.

***

My mother had whipped up a great meal, and a lot of people joined us for dinner. My brother and his wife lived with us for the summer. My father, Don Jamieson (his younger former partner and now the chief judge), and Gotty had all driven down together. Wilt and I joined them at the table along with my mother and sister.

After we ate, my father suggested that we all walk over to the local miniature golf course and play a round. Don, who was a single-digit golfer, loved the idea. The place was called Margate Miniature Golf and was only about five blocks from our house.

It was like a second home to me because earlier in the summer, my father had handed me a big stack of free passes. Apparently, he and the owner had something going on. I started playing there a lot, but most of the time, they wouldn't even take my pass. Soon, I knew every wrinkle in the carpet of every single hole.

It was just the men, and when we got there, Wilt suggested that we play a doubles match. He and I would be one team, and my brother and Don would be the other. My father and Gotty would watch from the sidelines.

The course was located on the corner of two large streets. Things were routine through the first three holes. The fourth had a trick to it, and I had reached the point where I could always get a hole-in-one there. You had to bank the ball off this one spot on a side bumper, and it would go right in. I knew exactly how it broke and had done it a million times.

When it was my turn, I made my usual shot. The ball hit the perfect spot, then made a slight turn and dropped into the cup. The large crowd spontaneously erupted into an enthusiastic round of applause.

"Crowd? What crowd?" I thought. The noise caught me completely by surprise. I looked up and saw we were surrounded by a mob of people. They were standing about four-deep on both streets, and there must have been a few hundred of them, all watching the game. The rest of the course had been closed for the occasion, and we were now the whole show.

"Good shot, man," Wilt said to me, slapping me lightly on the back.

"Oh right," I thought to myself. "Of course. The Wilt thing." I had forgotten about the Wilt thing. I had been away from it for a while. The course was empty when we got there, but now we were playing our match in front of a big crowd that was hanging on every shot. It shook me for a second, but I got used to it pretty fast. I had to.

That's the last thing I remember about the golf part of the night. Somehow, I was able to keep my composure and I'm pretty sure Wilt and I won the match.

The next thing I remember is that my father, Gotty, Mike, Don, Wilt, and I started to make the five-block walk back to our house. At least a hundred people followed along with us. A constant banter went on between Wilt and the crowd. There was a lot of laughter and everybody loved it. When we got near our house, my mother popped out on the porch to see what all the commotion was about.

"Clare," Gotty called to her. "I think you better put up another pot of spaghetti."

We turned the corner, and the Bentley was parked right there. "Wilt, can I get an autograph?" somebody called out.

He took a quick look at the crowd and looked over at my father as if to ask him what he thought. My father looked back at him as if to say—it's all right with me if it's all right with you.

"Sure," Wilt said to the kid and walked over to the Bentley. Suddenly, somehow, everybody was able to find a piece of paper. Wilt stood there for about an hour, using the roof of his car to sign autographs. He moved along at a leisurely pace, chatting with each person as he signed. A couple of flashbulbs went off, and everybody had a great time.

When he finished, my father looked at the crowd. "OK, everybody," he said to them. "Great to see you, but it's past the big guy's bedtime."

Wilt faked a huge yawn, and everybody laughed. He walked up the steps, waved to everyone, and went inside.

"Thanks for coming," my father said to the crowd as they started to leave. "And don't forget, come on out to the games. This is gonna be our year, everybody. Trust me, the Celtics and the rest of the league won't know what hit 'em."

26

The Plan Changes

The next day, as I thought about my car ride with Wilt, I realized that my father might have set the whole thing up. In retrospect, it seemed a bit contrived. Wilt had come down early, by himself. And as soon as we said hello, the next thing I knew, we were driving around alone together, and he started giving me a detailed pregnancy prevention seminar.

If my father had done it, I had to hand it to him. It was a pretty cool way to make sure I had all the information I needed to keep me out of trouble. It wasn't necessary, though. I had been going to overnight camp for nine years, and other than sports, all we ever talked about in the bunk was sex. And besides, as heated as our interludes ever got, my girlfriend and I were always careful to keep things out of the danger zone.

But now, it looked like things might be about to heat up a bit. There was a chance I could be getting the house all to myself for a few days. Although the idea was incredibly exciting, unfortunately, it was for a sad reason.

My mother's uncle, Uncle George, had gotten critically ill and was failing. He probably had less than a week to live. That meant a funeral was coming up, and it would be in Brooklyn. My parents would go, but they wouldn't take me. I never went to funerals. They thought I was still too young.

As Uncle George kept slipping away, I went over the situation in my mind. My parents would be gone for at least a full day, probably two. My brother and sister were both already back in Philadelphia. He was getting ready for his last year of law school and her college classes were about to begin. All I had to do was come up with a reason why I had to stay down the shore, which shouldn't be too hard.

I could hardly wait. My girlfriend and I had been limited to the back seats of cars, the beach, or anywhere else we could sneak in our steamy escapades. But now, finally we'd have the whole house to ourselves.

A couple of days later, my mother got the bad news. Uncle George was gone. My parents and I sat down for dinner that night, and, of course, the mood was somber.

I had only seen Uncle George a few times in my life. He was from my grandparents' generation and lived in Brooklyn. But he had been very close to my parents and I could see the deep sorrow on my mother's face. A big part of me definitely felt sad.

But I had another part that was equally as big, and it had just popped the cork on the champagne bottle. My imagination was already drunk.

In my mind, there I was, walking out of the dining room into the living room. But I was wearing a suave, white tuxedo, just like James Bond. And I was carrying two martinis. I had no idea what a martini was, but those glasses were so cool, whatever was in them had to be good.

My girlfriend sat on the couch wearing a black, low-cut evening gown, a long string of pearls lazily draped around her elegant neck. She crossed her shapely legs and dangled a black high-heeled shoe off the end of one foot. I handed her a martini. She took it and moistened her lips with her tongue. Then she brought the goblet up to her mouth. Oh, man, this was going to be great.

"Duv?" I heard my mother's voice calling to me, from somewhere beyond the fairy dust. "Duvid, are you OK?"

I was still waist-deep in my dream world and must have looked pretty distracted. "We know how hard it is," she said sympathetically. My parents had a quick conversation in Yiddish. And then the killer came.

"Duv, we think it's time—we think you should come with us to this one," my mother finally said.

"Huh?" I grunted. I heard exactly what she said, and I knew what it meant, but I hoped like hell I had gotten it wrong.

"To the funeral, to Uncle George's funeral," she explained. "We talked it over, and we think you're old enough now. You really should come with us. It's time."

I thought my head was going to explode. "Oh no! Oh my God, no!" I shouted silently. "This can't be happening!" But as I looked at them, I knew immediately that I would be going. There was no question about it. End of story. Dream dead.

I kept a calm, pensive expression as if considering the wisdom of the idea, but I was devastated. A moment earlier, I was one step away from Romance Heaven. Now, instead of being alone in the house with my girlfriend, doing God knows what, I'd be sitting in a long car ride up to Brooklyn with my parents, driving to my first funeral. I knew there was no way around it and reluctantly, my imagination switched from sex to death.

"Listen, Shortstop. I know how upset you must be," my father said. A master of the double entendre, he really knew how to say things without saying them. I realized that he probably knew exactly what I was planning to do with the house. In fact, I'm sure he knew it long before I did.

"But this is a perfect one for you to go to," he continued. "It's exactly right for you now. You were close enough to Uncle George that it matters, but not so close that it's gonna be a killer. It's always a good idea to get one of these under your belt before you have to go through a big one, you know what I mean? One that really hurts."

It was obvious what he was referring to. His parents, my beloved grandparents, were getting older. Before too long, they'd both be gone. I had to accept it; going to this funeral made perfect sense. For a lot of good reasons, it was definitely the right thing for me to do. And besides, I had no choice.

The next morning, as we started off for Brooklyn, both my parents were solemn. They had long, fond memories of Uncle George, and also, he was the last member of his generation to go. That always adds an extra dimension to a death. Now your generation becomes the oldest in the family. And every time someone goes, it hits you on a deeper level than before... that in reality, the bell tolls for thee.

It was a quiet ride. But as we got closer to Brooklyn, my father began instructing me on the process of burying someone you love. He explained what a funeral home was, what would happen when we got there, what it would probably be like at the cemetery, and what would happen at the shiva back at the house.

We pulled up to the funeral home, went inside, and were greeted by a large group of relatives from my mother's side of the family. We all hung around together for a few minutes. We didn't get to see each other all that often, so we couldn't help being glad, but it was obviously for the wrong reason. It's amazing how much like a party a funeral is, only it's not.

We all went in and sat in the middle rows. I could see the lid of the open coffin over the heads of the people sitting in front of us. According to my father's instructions, I knew that soon we'd walk past it, and I would see a dead person for the first time. I started to prepare myself.

"It's not really real yet," my father muttered in my ear. "Maybe it's a mistake. Maybe it's even a dream. But when you go up there, and you look in and you see him, and you know it's really him, then it's real. Then you know it's over."

"OK, Ike, let's go," my mother said to him. I felt him stiffen a little. Emotionally, everybody knew she was fifty times tougher than he was.

"Yeah," he said with a sigh. "Yeah. OK."

I braced myself for whatever was next. We stood up and went to the front of the room. We walked up to the coffin, and I looked in to see what was left of Uncle George.

It wasn't nearly as bad as I thought it would be. He didn't even look real. Actually, he looked like a figure in the wax museum on the boardwalk. Still, it was clearly him, and he was clearly dead. My father linked his arm in mine as we stood there staring at the lifeless form. "Now it's over," he said quietly.

We went back to our seats, and the service began. The rest of the day was uneventful—a standard funeral followed by a burial at a huge cemetery. Then, we headed back to the house for a couple of hours with some of our favorite relatives. That was the nice part of a rather sad day.

On the ride home, once we hit the Jersey Turnpike, I felt pretty good. I had gotten one under my belt, and it really wasn't all that bad.

27

Safety in His Atmosphere

Soon after the funeral, we moved back to Elkins Park from the shore. It was time to get ready for school and the upcoming 76ers season. My father had stepped up his efforts to find Wally Jones. The Bullets guard hadn't shown up for training camp, and nobody had any idea where he was. The papers said his legal problems had gotten worse.

My father opened talks with Baltimore about a possible trade. He also asked Vince Miller to get involved. Vince was Wilt's best friend. They had grown up together, in the same neighborhood as Wally, and they had all gone to Overbrook High.

Vince was a popular figure throughout the city and was extremely well-connected. He'd also become very tight with my father and although he wasn't officially with the team, he was around a lot. Gotty thought my father was grooming him to take a position in the front office soon, and then, at some point, possibly take over the top spot.

Vince went to work, but after ten days, there was still no news. Even so, my father decided to roll the dice. On September 22, 1965, he made a trade with the Bullets and got the rights to Wally Jones, who was still missing.

The papers were critical. According to them, Jones's life was in shambles and he was now an actual fugitive from justice. Nobody knew if he was still in the country or even if he was still alive, for that matter.

Finally, Vince got some news. He told my father he thought he knew where Jones was hiding and might be able to get a message to him. My father said to tell Wally that he had looked into his legal problems and was certain he could take care of them all. He wanted Wally to get in touch with him as soon as possible. Everything would be alright once he let my father go to work for him. The word went out.

The following Saturday, as I was having our usual after-synagogue lunch with my parents, the front doorbell rang. I got up to get it. When I opened the door, a disheveled twenty-something black guy was standing there with a small suitcase in his hand. He looked like a bum.

"Is this Ike Richman's house?" he asked me.

"Yeah," I said, mildly apprehensive.

"Is he here? My name's Wally Jones. I heard he might be able to help me."

"Sure," I said. "Hold on a second." I went and told my father, who dropped everything and came right to the door.

"Hello, Mr. Richman," Wally said, extending his hand. "I'm not sure if I—"

"Wally, great to see you," my father said, shaking his hand. "I'm so glad you came. Good choice! Come on in!"

They looked at each other for a brief moment. "Now, listen," my father said, getting right to the point. "I know all about your situation. I've looked into it thoroughly, and it's really not all that bad. We can definitely take care of it."

Wally looked surprised as if things had gotten off to

a much rosier start than he had hoped.

"Come on back, and let's have a talk," my father said, putting his hand on Wally's shoulder. He led him down the hallway toward his office. I heard the door close, and that always meant business.

But from his tone, I knew immediately that everything was going to be all right. I'd seen this kind of thing all my life. People would come to him in trouble and they would leave relieved.

My father had a great reputation as a brilliant problem solver, with a real genius for finding creative solutions that worked for everyone. He was also an astute judge of character, with wit, charm and an intelligent sense of humor. And he had a renowned soft touch. He would put people at ease, and then appeal to their better natures.

And most importantly, they felt safe with him. He had an unmistakable aura of power and authority, and intuitively, you knew you could trust him. If you had a serious problem, he was definitely the guy you wanted to see.

I had been planning to go out that afternoon to play ball with some friends, but I decided to wait until the meeting with Wally was over. This was a huge deal. Stories about him had dominated the news for weeks. Everybody knew if we got him, it would be a major coup. And at that moment, there were only three people in the whole world who knew what was going on, and I was one of them. I wasn't going anywhere.

I had some homework to do over the weekend, so I got my papers together and set myself up at the kitchen table. I could see the door to my father's office from there.

I took out my psychology homework. It was the first lesson of the year, and we were studying the basic human emotions of fear and safety. The assignment was to describe two recent times when you felt real fear, and then explain what happened that made you feel safe again.

The teacher was a super creative guy who ended up becoming an intellectual hippie. As a prompt, he had given us a statement Frederick Douglass made when he was asked what it was like to be around Abraham Lincoln. With elegant simplicity, he replied, "There was safety in his atmosphere."

This was going to be an easy assignment for me because the two major brushes I'd had with fear were still very fresh in my mind.

The first was at the beginning of that summer when one of my friends and I were on our way to a Phillies game. It was early evening, and we were in his family's small convertible, just the two of us. The weather was warm, and we had a few more hours of daylight, so we put the top down.

We drove down Broad Street, and when we got to North Philadelphia, there were far more people on the sidewalks than usual. Most of them were black, and they were walking south, the same direction we were driving.

It got unnerving because there had just been some serious racial unrest in the country, and things seemed to be getting more and more tense. As it happened, the LA Watts riots broke out only a week later and over thirty people died. And the neighborhood we were driving through had been the scene of a nasty street riot the previous summer when three hundred people were hospitalized.

As we drove on, the crowds got thicker, and I kept getting more uncomfortable. I don't trust big crowds. I had been going to ball games all my life and I knew how quickly things can get out of hand. It can turn ugly in a flash, and once it starts, it's almost impossible to stop.

People were everywhere, traffic had slowed to a

crawl and we had no idea what was going on. But we did know one thing. We were completely exposed—two white, affluent suburban teens sitting in an opened convertible, surrounded by hundreds of black people. Under the wrong circumstances, we would be sitting ducks.

But at the same time, I noticed something unusual. People were everywhere, but it was extremely quiet. In fact, it was almost silent. We were driving down Broad Street, which is a bustling six-lane avenue that runs the entire length of the city, and I don't think I even heard a horn honk. As we headed south, I could see that a famous church was the focus of the crowd. Everyone was walking toward it.

Once we finally got close enough where I could see what was really going on, I knew immediately that we were safe. Dr. Martin Luther King Jr. was standing on the church's front landing, and everyone was staring at him. He wasn't giving a speech or anything. There wasn't even a microphone or podium. He was just standing there, standing for what he stood for. And everyone else was standing along with him. The moment was filled with unity, commitment, and nobility. Nothing bad was going to happen.

King had been touring the country, trying to cool everybody out, and had been on a two-day visit to the city. He had just spoken in the church. There wasn't nearly enough room for everyone, so after he finished, he came out to be with the people who couldn't get in. By a wonderful twist of fate, we just happened to be driving by at that exact moment and got to witness it.

As I sat at the kitchen table, I jotted down some quick notes for the essay. People can have a tremendous effect on each other. Here, one person had brought out the best in thousands, just by his immense moral authority.

My fear had been that the crowd might have turned angry, which would have put us in serious danger. But instead, the opposite had happened—it was inspiring. There was certainly safety in his atmosphere.

I put down my pen and looked over at the door to my father's office. It was still closed. I decided to use the bathroom. It shared a wall with the office, so maybe I could hear something in there. When I went in, I heard my father and Wally's muffled voices, but I couldn't make out their words. Still, it was obvious they were into some pretty heavy stuff.

28

Give It to Me

I returned to the kitchen and got back to work. My second brush with fear had been quite different from the first. This one had real, in-your-face intensity. It happened when I had gotten into my first car accident a few months earlier.

I had inherited a beat-up sports car that had been handed down from my brother to my sister to me. It was a 1959 Austin-Healey Sprite, the famous "bug-eyed" model.

Gotty had picked it up for my brother on one of his trips to Europe. It was brand-new, white as a cloud, and the incarnation of pure fun. My brother kept it in perfect condition and drove me everywhere in it.

When he got married three years later, it went to my sister. My parents told her she could spruce it up, so Sybil had it painted jet-black with a red-and-white racing stripe down the back. She took off in it like a bat out of hell and drove it nonstop for the next three years. By her second year at Temple, she had outgrown it. It was only a two-seater and didn't work for her anymore. So as soon as I got my license, it came to me.

Now, they say that when a first baby drops its

pacifier on the floor, the parents sanitize it in boiling water. With their second baby, if the pacifier falls on the floor, they rinse it off with hot water. And with the third baby, if the pacifier falls on the floor, they just let the dog lick it. By the time I got the Sprite, it had clearly been to the dogs. But I loved it.

It had a manual four-speed stick shift. I had been driving it for about two weeks and hadn't quite gotten the hang of it yet, but I was getting there. One sunny afternoon, as I was out driving, I pulled into the parking lot behind some stores. I was trying to turn around but had trouble getting it into reverse and was stuck there.

All of a sudden, a big car—an older Buick—backed up and smashed right into me. The jolt of the accident and the sound of shattering glass shook me to the core. I got out to take a look. The front-left side was mangled and bent, and the headlight was smashed.

I looked at the dark-green Buick, which was the size of a tank, and it didn't even have a scratch. Then the car door opened, and my worst nightmare got out—a tough-looking, lanky hoodlum with a lit cigarette in his mouth and a mean snarl on his face. He didn't really look all that human.

"What da fucksa matter with you, dude?" he growled furiously. As he walked toward me, I thought he was about to hit me.

The parking lot was behind Kelley's Bar, which was one of the seedier establishments in the township. It was about four-thirty in the afternoon and the guy smelled like he'd been drinking for hours.

I was too shocked and scared to say anything, so I just stood there staring at him. He must have concluded that I was no threat, and he relaxed a little.

"Tough shit, kid," was the next pearl of wisdom that came out of his mouth. "Too bad you hit me. Now, what do you want to do about it?"

"I hit you?" I asked, finding enough strength to speak. "I didn't hit you. I couldn't even get the car into reverse. I was just sitting there. You backed into me."

The hoodlum chuckled, took a leisurely drag from his cigarette, and blew out a long stream of liquor-laced, gray smoke into my face.

"You know that, and I know that," he said. "But we're the only ones who do. You see anybody else here? No. It's just me and you. So, the truth is gonna be what I say it is. And when we go in front of the judge, the truth is that you hit me. You got that, asshole?"

He had a mean smile on his hard face, and it was clear that he was starting to enjoy himself. The cruelty of it took my panic to a new level. Like a stunned rabbit in the grip of a python, I could feel the coils tightening around me.

I don't remember how I did it, but I got him to write his name and number down on a piece of paper. I'm pretty sure it was on the back of a racing form. There was a horse track about ten miles away.

I got back into the Sprite and drove home. It still moved, but it was a shaky mess as it rattled along. I backed into the garage, so my father could see the damage. I shut the engine off, and to my surprise, I burst into tears. I cried like I was six instead of sixteen. I couldn't believe I could still fall apart that easily. I thought I was much more grown-up than that. It didn't really matter. I knew my back was against the wall and the situation was hopeless.

About an hour later, when my father came home from work, I was sitting at the kitchen table waiting for him. I did my best to keep it together as I told him what had happened. We went right out into the garage to take a look.

As we both stared at the crumpled side of the car and the smashed headlight, I started giving him the details. I was fine until I got to the part when the guy said he was going to make me lie to the judge in court. At that point, I got choked up.

I tried to go on, but my father simply held up his right hand, signaling me to stop talking. In his stillness, he looked like a mighty Indian chief who had stopped time.

"Did you, uh, happen to get any information from this guy?" he asked quietly. "You know what I mean? His name, his phone number? Anything like that?"

His tone was completely calm and ordinary, and it surprised me. Instead of being rattled by this horrible situation, he sounded like we were sitting at a casual lunch and he was asking me to pass him the salt. It was nothing to him, which did something to me.

"Sure," I responded and pulled the crumpled racing form out of my pocket.

"Give it to me," he said simply and extended his right hand. There was no emotion in his voice and no expression on his face, but there was also no question about what was going on. I was face to face with the enormous, unmistakable power that was firmly and forever on my side. Nothing was going to hurt me.

I put the paper in his hand, and as soon as he took it, the weight of the world was lifted off my shoulders and I could breathe again. He looked at the information.

"OK," he said. "Here's what's gonna happen. You're just going to take the car over to a place called Frese and Fishers in town, and they'll handle it. Frese and Fishers."

I tried to concentrate and remember the name, but it flew right out of my mind.

"You know what? Don't worry about it," he said, sensing I was struggling. "Just call my office tomorrow morning, and Bernadette will take care of the whole thing." He put his hand on my shoulder and held it there, as steady as a mountain and as reassuring as the dawn.

"OK?" he asked me, looking in my eyes for the all-clear. I nodded to him. "OK," he said with finality, indicating that the episode was over.

"Enough already!" he exclaimed. "Come on. Let's go back inside."

We left the garage. He put his arm around my shoulder, and with synchronized steps, we walked back to the house. As we approached the kitchen window, I could see my mother through the glass, working at the sink. She lifted her head, and as a Madonna Amongst the Dishes, with a subtle Mona Lisa smile, she gazed sublimely at the sight of her youngest child, walking along the path, under the shelter and protection of his father.

Once we were inside and he started down the hall to his office, he called back to me. "Don't worry about this, Duv. It's no big deal."

And it wasn't. I called his secretary in the morning, and she told me exactly what to do. She had already set up the appointment, and the body shop treated me royally. Within another day, the car was fine, and I was driving it as though nothing had ever happened. I never heard another word about it again.

I started making some notes for the essay. I realized that in my extreme fear, it had never occurred to me that my father might have been able to help. In fact, I forgot I even had a father.

But in truth, he was one of the most powerful attorneys in the city, his protégé was the President Judge of the Philadelphia Court System and his partner was the

Police Commissioner of Cheltenham Township. So, in reality, that half-drunk degenerate who had threatened me in the bar's parking lot, had no power over me at all. But try explaining that to sheer terror.

Still, everything had changed the instant my father had taken that nicotine-stained racing form out of my hand. Light had dispelled darkness, I noted, reflecting on the incident. It was as simple as that.

Now suddenly the door to my father's office opened, and Wally stepped out, with my father right behind him. I closed my notebook and followed them into the hall but hung back and watched. I don't think they even noticed me.

They had only known each other for an hour, but you could've sworn they were old friends. Wally still looked dirty and disheveled, but he certainly didn't look like a bum anymore. My father walked him to the opened door and put his arm around his shoulder.

"Now, this is all going to be OK, Wally. I promise you we can handle it. It's time to put the whole thing behind you."

"I'll do that, Mr. Richman," Wally said. "I will."

"Call me first thing Monday morning," my father said. "And don't forget, the important thing now is to get back in the game and start working on your jump shot. You gotta get that rust off."

They both chuckled. Wally walked out to his car, and my father turned to me, with the smile of a job well done. I'd seen that look of his a million times.

***

A few days later, the 76ers announced that Wally Jones had come back to Philly and had joined the team. Amazingly, all his legal problems were quickly resolved, and the whole city was buzzing with anticipation.

When he met the reporters after his first practice, he said, "I think my problems are more mental than physical, and Mr. Richman already has helped me see some sunshine for the first time in a long while. I have a little peace of mind for the first time in three years, and I want a chance to show the world what I can do."

Soon, he would do just that. And along with the recent signing of Billy Cunningham, my father's dream team was complete.

Billy, the great star from the University of North Carolina, was his number-one draft pick. He and my father had grown quite fond of each other, but contractually, they had hit a snag.

My father had offered Billy $12,000 for the year. But Billy wanted $12,500 and was holding out. Neither one would budge. Finally, right before the season was about to begin, my father threw in the towel and gave Billy the extra five hundred.

Now everything was in place, and we were ready to begin the new season. And our quest for destiny.

Part 3

29

Einstein's Eyes

With Wally Jones and Billy Cunningham, my father's vision for the 76ers was complete. Wilt was now surrounded by championship-caliber team players, so opponents couldn't focus on just trying to stop him. We were ready to go.

In those days, the pre-season began in October and all the games were exhibitions, except for the ones on the last three Saturday nights of the month, which all counted on the record.

The first league game was in Baltimore and we blew them out by 32 points. The next Saturday night, Detroit came to Philly, and we crushed them by 17. Then the following Saturday night, Cincinnati came, and they could barely stay on the court with us. We clobbered them by 20.

The press went nuts. The team was "destined for greatness" and "on the verge of the championship." And we were only three games into the season.

The whole city was in love, but now it was personal. Chet Walker was "Chet the Jet." Wally Jones became "Wally Wonder." Hal Greer was "High Gear." Billy Cunningham was "Billy C" or "The Kangaroo Kid." And the two big men were known by just their first names. Luke Jackson was almost biblically, "Luke." And of course, Wilt was just plain "Wilt." But that was nothing new. Nobody else ever had that name.

***

The regular season began in November, which was going to be a busy month for our family. Along with seventeen 76ers games, we also had three major social events, planned for the last three Sundays of the month. First, there was an Israeli Bonds dinner in honor of my father. Then, the following week, my parents were hosting an engagement party for my sister and her fiancé. And on the last Sunday, there would be a smaller party for my mother's fiftieth birthday.

For the team, things started with a rough road trip. We had four games in four straight nights and we lost three of them, including a stinging loss to the Celtics in The Garden.

But the next week, the week leading up to the Bond dinner, we came home and got hot. We beat LA and San Francisco each by 8 points. And then on Friday night, we had a rematch with the Celtics. But this time, it was in our own madhouse, Convention Hall.

The intense battle started out dead even, but we broke it open early and turned it into a romp. We trounced them in front of an ecstatic sold-out crowd, and the series with them was now tied at 1–1.

Saturday night, we went up to New York and beat the Knicks soundly. So now we were on a strong winning streak, which set a great tone for the celebratory Bond dinner the next night, Sunday, November 14.

***

About three hundred people came to the auditorium at Temple Sholom for the event. It was sponsored by the State of Israel, in recognition of my father's years of service as the Israeli Bonds redemption chairman for the Mid-Atlantic Region. His critical volunteer job was to collect the money that had been pledged and make sure it got where it was supposed to go. It was always a top priority for him.

The Mayor of Philadelphia was an honorary chairman, along with a popular comedian named Joey Bishop, who was a big star at the time. Friends with Frank Sinatra, Dean Martin, and Sammy Davis Jr. he was an original member of the famous "Rat Pack."

Joey was one of my father's early-childhood friends from South Philly. His real name was Joey Gottlieb, and my father had given him his first job in show business. Joey and his brothers had a singing/comedy act, and my father had booked them at the small resort hotel he owned in the Pocono Mountains. It was the first time the act ever played professionally. After that, Joey went out on his own and moved to LA, where his career really took off. He and my father stayed in touch and my father visited him whenever he went out there.

One thing about my father—no matter where he was in the world, he went to synagogue every Saturday morning. Once in LA, Joey took him to his place, and Sammy Davis Jr. joined them. My father was really impressed with him. He said his conversion to Judaism was real, he was very serious about the religion, and he sang all the prayers perfectly. At the end of the service, they hugged each other, and I'm sure for my father it was quite a "Shabbat Sholom."

At the Bond dinner, I was seated at a table with a bunch of people I didn't know. My mother had spread all the kids around to make it more of a mixture. The man who was sitting next to me was about my father's age, and he introduced himself to me as Henry Abrams.

The evening began on a high note when they called my grandfather up to the dais to sing the blessings. He performed the standard ones over the wine and bread. And then he added a rare benediction given by a father to his child on a special occasion. Zayde's voice was at its peak, and he put all his heart and soul into it, especially the stirring ending. Everyone was deeply moved as they said the traditional "Amen."

My father got up and walked over to shake his hand. But when he did, Zayde grabbed him and gave him a big hug, holding him in a long embrace. My father seemed to break up a little and everyone spontaneously rose, giving them a heartfelt standing ovation.

When we sat down, the man next to me leaned over, put his hand on my arm and said, "I gotta tell you a story about your Zayde. It's important."

My mother told me about this guy later. He was Dr. Henry Abrams, a renowned ophthalmologist from Princeton, and he had been Albert Einstein's eye doctor, as well as a good friend. After Einstein died, his brain and eyes were preserved for scientific research. In Princeton, Dr. Abrams was an acknowledged genius and was given Einstein's eyes to study.

"Your father was one of my best friends at Temple when we were in college," he said to me, once things settled down. "After we graduated, he went to law school, and I went to med school, but your grandfather's house was always our home base. We were there all the time.

"One day, it must have been around 1935, we were eating lunch, and your grandfather came bursting in like a raving maniac. We thought he had lost his mind. He was screaming and yelling—really going nuts. Your father tried to calm him down, but it was impossible.

"Apparently, the United States was trying to decide whether or not to compete in the Olympics, which were being held in Berlin the next year. People were concerned, but your grandfather was carrying on like it was the end of the world.

"Now, you have to understand something. This was four years before the war. Germany was still a civilized country, and a lot of people in England, Europe, and even America liked Hitler. Nobody had any idea of what was going to happen."

As Dr. Abrams stopped and took a drink of water, the brilliant diamond in his pinky ring sparkled in the light. There was definitely something unusual about him. I don't know if it was the perfect dome of his bald head or the glow in his eyes, but there was an aura of wisdom about him, and I felt privileged to be in his company.

"Anyway, we couldn't understand why your grandfather was so upset, but we couldn't calm him down," he explained. "At one point, your father tried to reason with him, but he slammed his fist down on the table, and shouted, 'You don't understand who this guy Hitler is. I'm telling you—he's going to kill every Jew he can get his hands on.'"

Dr. Abrams got quiet and retreated into his own world for a moment. "David," he said finally, "Listen to me. Your father and grandfather are two very special men. I've known them for thirty-five years and believe me - you are one fortunate soul to have been born into their care."

Dinner was soon served. After dessert, Connecticut Senator John Pastore, who had come up from Washington, delivered the keynote speech. He then introduced my father, who spoke briefly and ended by suggesting to the senator that he sponsor a bill making Israel the fifty-first state.

The audience got a big laugh out of it, but my father didn't seem to be kidding. Along with everybody else in the room, he took the security of the State of Israel extremely seriously.

As I looked around the room at the men in their tuxedos and the women in their formal gowns—all happy, healthy, and successful-looking people—I remembered the hollow faces of the emaciated concentration-camp survivors from the newsreels. And it hit me how thin the line was that separated them. Maybe just a few bad decisions, a few wrong choices by their elders, and some of the people in this room would have gone down that same horrible road.

They had lived through extremely harrowing times, and it wasn't all that long ago. Less than twenty years had passed since two-thirds of the Jewish population of Europe had been murdered during the war. And then, soon after, once the Jewish State had been declared, it was immediately attacked by an axis of five powerful neighbors, all sworn to its annihilation. Only by a slim miracle, had Israel been able to survive.

To me, all this stuff was history. Like the Civil War or the Declaration of Independence, it was just part of a bygone era. But to the people at the dinner, it was different. It wasn't some dead history from a book, it was living in their memory. Israel's need for survival was in their blood. And they always put their money where their hearts were.

As the formal part of the program ended, it was followed by a long social period. Then the evening finally drew to a close. Partly because it had been a fundraiser, my parents stood together by the door, thanking each person individually as they left.

I sat by myself in the back of the room, in my usual spot under the mural of Joseph, and watched them. Everyone's face was filled with love, admiration, and respect for both of them. The whole evening had been a beautiful occasion. And somehow, it had seemed so right.

30

Time to Focus

The next week, the 76ers played five games in six days, and it was a rough stretch. After winning the first one, they dropped three in a row. But then, on national TV, they clobbered the Lakers in LA, which lifted our spirits in time for the big engagement party my parents were hosting for my sister and her fiancé.

It was a Sunday afternoon, just one week after the Bond dinner, and our house was filled with family and friends. Sybil was engaged to a promising young man she had met at camp. They had continued their relationship through college, even though he was in DC and she was in Philly.

My parents were thrilled and were pulling out all the stops for the party. They couldn't have been happier. Not only was she their only daughter, but the "wild Indian" finally seemed to be settling down. Instead of marrying some motorcycle-riding, black-leather-jacketed rebel without a cause, which could have easily happened, she had fallen in love with a fine, upstanding law student—and a handsome Jewish one, at that. My father already had plans for him in the firm.

At one point early in the party, I was hanging out in the front hall with my brother, Gotty, Zink, and one of their contemporaries, a white-haired old-timer named Eddie Newborn.

A real character, Newborn, as everybody called him, was the CEO of Convention Hall. Besides being the home of the 76ers, it was also Philadelphia's premier performance venue. Every big act in show business played there, and Newborn always had plenty of great seats. So, in a very real way, he was one of the most powerful men in the city.

And inside Convention Hall, there was nothing he couldn't do. Once, world-renowned violinist Itzhak Perlman was booked to play there, and Koz's son, who had just gotten married, wanted to take his bride to the concert. It had been sold out for a year, all the standing room tickets were long gone, and there was absolutely nothing left. No problem for Newborn. He sat them on the stage itself, with two chairs off to the side, behind the curtain. Everyone was amazed, but to him, it was no big deal. All in a day's work.

He and Gotty went way back, and as we all stood together, they were like two hard-boiled Borscht Belt comedians, trading sardonic barbs about everything and everyone.

At one point, the front door opened, and Sybil's lifelong friend, Nina, came in with by her boyfriend. They walked past us, and Newborn followed them with his eyes. Then he looked back with a goofy expression and asked, "Who's zat? Sonny and Cher?"

We all cracked up, because Sonny and Cher had just played Convention Hall the night before. Their pictures had been all over the place for weeks, so we all knew what they looked like. And at first glance, this strange-looking couple could have easily been them.

They had the same look which, for the time, was

clearly off-the-wall. Cher wore dark, heavy eye makeup and she had thick bangs, with long, straight black hair that went all the way down to her waist. And Sonny looked like a long-haired, jolly caveman who had been cleaned-up and decked-out in a hippie outfit.

We were in a conservative Republican suburb, and these two stuck out like a sore thumb. Of course, everyone was polite, but nobody had ever seen anything like them in real life before.

Nina and I actually had some history together. She was one of Sybil's oldest friends, and I knew her well. When we moved to our new house, she lived only a block away. Although she and Sybil had been close before, now she was over all the time and our place was like a second home to her.

One night, early in ninth grade, I had left one of my schoolbooks in Sybil's room and had to go in and get it. I started down the hall, and of course, her door was closed. But I could hear the sound of this hillbilly singer that she liked. She had one of his records and played it constantly.

He had a high, twangy voice and accompanied himself on the guitar and harmonica. I figured it must have been a comedy album. Why else would you pay money to listen to someone with a sound like that? It turned out it was Bob Dylan and he would become a major hero of mine. I would know all his songs by heart, but that was still a few years down the road.

I knocked on the door. Over the music, I heard Nina shout that I should come in. When I did, I was surprised to find that Sybil wasn't home.

Nina was sitting on the bed wearing a white oxford shirt with the sleeves rolled up to her elbows. A few opened books were spread out in front of her, and her hair was damp, like she had just gotten out of the shower. Her legs and feet were bare.

I had come in to get The Little Prince, a book we were reading in my French class. We had to read it in the original French, and I was getting nowhere. I'd been taking the language since fourth grade and I could say maybe four sentences in it.

Nina was a French major and fluent. I told her how much trouble I was having, and she offered to give me a hand. The next thing I knew, we were both sitting on the floor together. I started reading the book out loud, and she began explaining it to me, word by word.

I'm sure she was giving me a lot of helpful pointers, but I wasn't really paying attention. Whatever interest I had in The Little Prince evaporated as soon as we hit the floor. I was a red-blooded, fifteen-year-old boy, who was now sitting next to a half-naked, extremely attractive college girl. She had a lovely face and a perfect figure. And we were only inches apart. I had never been in a situation like that before and to top it off, she had just used some lilac hair conditioner and the scent of it was driving me up the wall.

As you learn in science, at a certain age, the male human body starts to manufacture extremely powerful reproductive hormones. Their main purpose is to ensure the survival of the species, and they generate an irresistible urge to reproduce that never stops.

It begins innocently enough, but as you grow, it keeps getting stronger. Before you know it, the hormones have taken over your entire being, both physical and mental. And from then on, the whole world is just one big conspiracy, designed to egg you on.

The concept is brilliant and has served our species for millions of years. For me, it had begun to kick in about a year earlier, and by the time I was inhaling the vapors of Nina's aura, the hormones owned me—lock, stock, and barrel. It would be forty years before I'd be able to think straight again.

Her bare legs were almost touching me, and that intoxicating scent of lilac rose up my nostrils and exploded into my brain with every breath I took. Meanwhile, her soft, ultra-feminine voice kept purring French in my ear.

I couldn't take it anymore and finally decided to get the hell out of there. It was the only sane thing to do. I abruptly told her I had to go, closed the incomprehensible book, and stood up.

She sat there smiling as if she understood completely. When I got to the door, I turned around for one last look. She was sitting there, staring out the window into the night and her beauty in the moonlight really threw me.

That lilac-drenched episode was less than two years before the engagement party. Now, as I looked into the living room, I could see her and Sybil laughing and sharing champagne together. She had just gotten engaged as well, and the two young women were full of smiles, getting ready for their bright futures.

So, this freshly showered vision of French loveliness had turned into a dead ringer for Cher. It was a shocking transformation. But we were only in the very beginning of a massive cultural revolution that would turn the whole world upside down. Of course, nobody knew it back then, but it was far more than just the times that were changing.

***

The next Sunday night, one week later, we had a small dinner party at our house for my mother's fiftieth birthday. It was just the immediate family and some close friends, including Gotty and Zink.

As the evening wore on, a few of us sat around the table and the talk turned to Wilt. Some recent newspaper stories had brought up the idea of him fighting Muhammad Ali for the heavyweight crown.

Gotty thought it was a great idea and was sure Wilt could beat him. My father refused to even discuss it. In his mind, there was no upside. If Wilt beat Ali, nobody would be impressed because of his overwhelming size advantage. But if he lost, it would be a disaster. He would be Goliath to Ali's David, and he'd be stuck with the loser image for the rest of his life. After a little more thought, Gotty agreed. He had tremendous respect for my father's business judgment. "Ike is a rare combination," he used to say. "You don't see it all that often – a really, really nice guy, who really, really knows how to get things done. Not only does he know everybody – he knows what they want."

Also, my father was troubled by the whole situation with Ali and the Black Muslims. In February 1964. Ali, whose original name was Cassius Clay, had beaten the reigning heavyweight champion, Sonny Liston. The day after he won, Clay announced that he had converted to Islam and was officially changing his name to Muhammad Ali. Someone named Malcolm X was standing next to him.

At the time, the Black Muslims were a largely unknown fringe group. They had a radical approach to race relations in America that was almost the opposite of the nonviolent teachings of Martin Luther King Jr., whose influence was the late Mahatma Gandhi.

At the fight's rematch in May 1965, nobody knew how the new champ was going to be introduced in the ring. Would they use his old name or his new one? The mainstream press still called him Cassius Clay, which infuriated him.

My father and I listened to the fight on the radio. After introducing Liston, the ring announcer said, "And now, in this corner, wearing white trunks, standing six feet three inches tall and weighing two hundred six pounds, the heavyweight champion of the world..."

He paused and then, barely able to pronounce the foreign name, hesitantly stuttered, "Moe-Hammd – Ahhh-Leee!"

"Jesus Christ!" my father said, slapping his forehead with the palm of his hand, which struck me as pretty funny. Here was a Jew, invoking the name of Christ in reaction to a converted Muslim—a real trifecta. My father wasn't smiling, though. He looked like he'd just heard the rumblings of a distant earthquake. Ali knocked Liston out in the first round, and the greatest spokesman for the controversial movement took the world stage.

Most people were upset about it, but Wilt never took it too seriously. He knew both Ali and Malcolm X pretty well. Harlem was the center of their universe, and Wilt owned one of its most important nightspots: Big Wilt's Smalls Paradise.

A neighborhood establishment since 1925, he bought it in 1961 and started keeping it open 24 hours a day. He became a major figure up there and visited the club as much as he could, often working up to 18 hours a stretch.

He really knew who-was-who and always claimed Malcolm X had been a waiter at his club, going by the alias "Detroit Red." I recognized the name a few years later in college, when we studied "The Autobiography of Malcolm X," a book that had a serious impact on me.

Wilt did have his concerns about some of the people involved in the movement. According to him, a few rough characters were in the mix, possibly a criminal element. True or not, unfortunately, the whole thing didn't end well for Malcolm.

As far as a boxing match with Ali was concerned, Wilt had no question that he could easily beat him. But the idea was mainly a ruse. He and Ali were somewhat friendly and over the years, they would play up the idea of having a fight, whenever either one of them wanted publicity. They both used that PR tactic more than once.

But in November of 1965, no matter what Wilt or anyone else thought, they knew better than to bring it up in front of my father. To him, it was just a distraction. And this was no time for distractions. It was time to focus. The championship was finally within our grasp.

We had a game in Baltimore on Tuesday, November 30. And then, on Friday, December 3, we had a critical showdown with the Celtics, back in Boston.

Each team had won easily on its home court and the series was tied, 1-1. Now, according to my father, it was time for us to make a major statement and show them and the rest of the world who we were. It was time to go up there and finally beat them in The Garden.

31

More Than You Know

Sometimes our lives can be unfolding normally and then something happens and suddenly your whole world is turned upside down. There's no point in dwelling on it, but the truth is, we never really know what's coming around the next corner in this life. Things can change in an instant and before you know it, nothing is the same, ever again. It seems to happen to everyone. Sooner or later, one way or another, we each enter into the dark night of the soul.

That's exactly where I was heading as the last week of November began. I didn't see it coming. We rarely do. But looking back, there were plenty of signs.

The first one was hardly noticeable. My brother's wife was about seven months pregnant. Mike had been the first child in the generation following my father's. Now this new baby would be the first child of the next generation. We were all unbelievably excited.

My father and I had driven over to visit them one afternoon. When we got home and pulled into the driveway, I asked him, "So how does it feel now that you're going to be a grandfather?"

"What do you mean?" he asked me.

"Does it make you feel old or anything?"

He didn't respond right away and stared out at the rose garden near the back door.

"I'm never going to be the grandfather to this child," he said matter-of-factly, but in a distant tone of voice. I didn't say anything.

"No. I won't be the grandfather," he repeated. "I'll be the father's father, but never the grandfather."

He used to say quirky things like this all the time. It sounded like he was splitting hairs, and I didn't pay any attention to it.

***

A second subtle omen came in the form of a comic book. Eleventh grade was turning out to be a great year for me. I was in student council and started thinking about running for school president. Cheltenham was a big high school, with about two thousand students. If I wanted to run, there would be a lot to do, and it was time to give it some serious thought. One night at dinner, I mentioned it to my parents and they both encouraged me.

The next day, when I got home from school, an old comic book of mine was on the end table next to my bed. It had stories about each president of the United States. I hadn't seen it in years. My mother kept a few boxes of my childhood things in the basement and had pulled it out after our dinner conversation, probably to inspire me.

I recognized it immediately and remembered there was a strange story about Abraham Lincoln in the middle of it. I flipped to the center and sure enough, there it was, "Lincoln, the Mystic."

It had two parts. The first one was called, "I Am

Not Dead – I Still Live." It showed a letter from a famous psychic that was found in Lincoln's desk after he died. Supposedly channeled, there was a life-after-death message from a close friend of Lincoln's who had been killed in battle. Written backwards, it had to be read in a mirror. It said—"I am not dead. I still live...I experienced a happy reality—a glorious change by the process called death... Man lives on Earth, to live elsewhere, and that elsewhere is ever present. Heaven and Hell are conditions, not localities."

The fact that Lincoln had a letter from a psychic in his desk was somewhat intriguing. But when I read the second part of the story, I found it disturbing. It was called "The Most Famous Pre-Cognitive Dream in American History."

It showed Lincoln asleep in the White House. A mournful sound wakes him up. He gets out of bed and starts walking toward it. As he gets closer, he realizes that it is the sound of people crying miserably. He enters the East Room and sees a coffin on a stand, guarded by soldiers. "Who is dead in the White House?" he asks one of them.

"The president," comes the reply. "He was killed by an assassin." The crying gets louder. Lincoln looks in the coffin and sees himself lying there. The shock of it startles him, and he suddenly wakes up and finds himself lying in his bed. He realizes it had all been a bad dream.

As I sat on my bed next to the end table, I looked at the image of Lincoln, staring at himself in the coffin, and for some reason, I thought of my old Davy Crockett comic book. I remembered how crushed I was when I realized my hero was dead, and I got a quick flash of the intense grief I felt back then. It jolted me like a shock wave and I quickly got up and put the comic away in a drawer. Still, that haunting image of Lincoln staring at his own dead body in the coffin stayed with me for quite a while.

***

A more profound portent awaited me on Saturday morning. My father and I were sitting in services in the modern synagogue near our home in Elkins Park. He was thinking about changing our affiliation. We still belonged to Temple Sholom, but it was a long drive each way. This place was close enough that we could walk, which was a dream come true for him.

Toward the end of every Jewish service, a prayer is recited called the Mourner's Kaddish. It's one of the keystones of the religion, and every congregation does it, all over the world. Interestingly, even though it's done to honor the dead, it's a prayer of praise and never once mentions death or dying. The idea is that you always praise God, no matter what happens.

As we sat there, the rabbi invited the mourners to rise to say Kaddish, and one of the kids from my school stood up, which surprised me. "I know that kid," I whispered to my father. "I didn't know anybody in his family died."

Suddenly, my father got extremely serious. "This Kaddish prayer is much more important than you know," he said. Then he spoke to me in a strange tone of voice, one I had never heard before. I could barely tell it was him.

"I want you to promise me that after I die, you will come to services and say Kaddish for me, every morning and every night. And that you will do it for the full eleven months and never miss a time."

I had never heard him that somber before, and it didn't make sense. I was definitely going to say Kaddish for him after he died, but that was twenty or thirty years

214

down the road—he was only fifty-two. "Of course, I will, Dad," I said matter-of-factly. "You know I will."

Then the weird got weirder. "We're in the synagogue now," he said, still in that same somber tone. "There's the ark and we're in front of the Torah. I want you to make a solemn vow to me now. And understand, this is a vow made before God."

Now, we were very close and nothing like this had ever happened between us. He had never asked me to promise him anything before in my life.

"OK," I said, somewhat taken aback. It seemed like an old-fashioned idea, but why not?

"Good," he said. "Now, repeat after me." He paused, and then, like a judge administering an oath of office, he recited the vow, one sentence at a time. And I repeated it after him, word for word.

"I promise before God, that after you die, I will come to services and say Kaddish for you every morning and night for the full eleven months. And never miss a time." When I said the last phrase, he exhaled deeply and slumped forward in his seat, with his eyes closed.

The next thing I knew, they started singing Adon Olam, which is the very last song of the service. It's a happy, cheerful hymn. My father opened his eyes and looked relieved. He seemed like his normal self again and started singing along. Whatever that strange spell was, it was over.

When we got outside, it was a beautiful day. On the walk home, we were both happy, I always loved that time after services on a Saturday. I had fulfilled my obligation to God and my father and now I could get on with the carefree part of my weekend.

32

You Have Come upon It

Two nights later, Monday night, I had a disturbing nightmare. Someone was trying to kill me. I was desperately running for my life on a deserted part of the beach in Atlantic City, in front of the boardwalk. It was daytime, but the atmosphere was dark and heavy, like a major storm was coming.

As I ran frantically, the would-be killer kept firing a gun at me. But the assailant, the gun, and the bullets were all invisible. Still, I could hear the loud crack of the gunfire and feel the sharp zing of the bullets as they whizzed past my head and exploded in the sand in front of me. The assassin was hell-bent on my destruction, relentless and getting closer all the time.

In sheer terror, I ran under the boardwalk to hide. But once I did, the whole scene changed immediately. I was standing in a dark cave and everything was completely silent. Before, when I was running for my life, I heard the panting of my breath, the thumping of my feet on the sand, and the hiss of the bullets as they flew past my head. Now everything was dead silent and absolutely still.

I was standing in front of an old, brown wooden

cross, with hundreds of lit candles all around. A monk in a dark-brown, hooded robe stood in front of it. The hood concealed the monk's face entirely.

"Behold! The cross of the Crucifixion!" I seemed to hear inside my mind. I knew it was somehow coming from the monk. Then oddly, a few complete understandings occurred to me. Unlike linear thinking, where one thought follows another, they became clear all at once.

I understood that this was the actual cross from the actual crucifixion and that things were serious. I knew that it was a symbol for death, commonly used to mark a grave. And the final message was—"You have come upon it." I looked at the monk, then back at the cross. Suddenly everything seemed frozen in time, like a picture. The candles had stopped flickering, and nothing moved. It was completely still, and the stillness seemed to have a presence all its own.

Then I felt a sharp slap in the middle of my chest, right on my sternum. I gasped in an enormous amount of air and the next thing I knew, I was lying in my bed, in my pajamas.

I was in my room, it was morning, and I realized it had all been a dream, a nightmare. My right hand was resting on my chest. I must have stopped breathing in my sleep and then subconsciously slapped myself awake.

I was pretty shaken and didn't move for a few minutes. I finally got up, got dressed, and had my breakfast. But as I started driving to school, I was still disturbed. I hardly ever had nightmares and certainly never anything like this before.

By the time I pulled into the school parking lot though, I was more relaxed and decided to let the whole thing go. After all, it was just a bad dream. Maybe it was something I ate. The rest of the day was uneventful, and everything seemed fine.

And it would have stayed fine, except that night, Tuesday, I had the same exact nightmare again, right down to the tiniest detail, through to the very end. Now I was rattled. This was more than just a nightmare, it was a recurring nightmare, which made it really weird.

Then, to my extreme shock and dismay, the next night, Wednesday, I had the exact same dream. Again, I was being chased along the beach by an invisible killer, firing invisible bullets at me. I ducked under the boardwalk, and it turned into a cave. There was the cross and the monk. And I got the same set of inner understandings, ending with the message—"You have come upon it." Then I slapped myself awake.

I didn't know what to do. Three straight nights of this recurring nightmare seemed really serious. And on top of that, the fact that it had a big cross in it was deeply disturbing. The truth is, I didn't like crosses. They always made me feel uncomfortable. And it wasn't due to any religious differences. It was much deeper than that, a visceral feeling, like getting punched in the stomach.

I felt it the very first time I saw a crucifixion scene, which was when I was about six. We still lived in the Northeast, across the street from the church and I was having a catch with a friend. The ball went over and landed near the front door of the building. When I went to get it, I noticed that the church door was opened. The place had always been mysterious to me, so I thought I'd go in and take a peek.

The first thing I saw in there was a huge cross with a lifelike porcelain statue of a nearly naked man nailed to it. The guy was dead. And there was a crown of sharp thorns stuck into his head, with blood streaming down his face.

Thorns! I couldn't believe it. My mother grew rose bushes and always warned me to be careful of them. Still, I got stuck in the finger once. It bled a lot and it really hurt. Seeing a bunch of thorns stuck in this poor guy's head was appalling. The rest of his body was a real horror show too, with whip marks all over it and nails hammered into his hands and feet.

It was the most gruesome sight I had ever seen in my life and it made me sick to my stomach. I ran out full speed, crossed the street and collapsed onto our lawn. My head was spinning, and I was out of breath. But the firm ground and familiar smell of the grass made me feel better. After a few minutes, I calmed down.

Then, out of nowhere, an unexpected fury came over me and I was filled with anger and rage. "Look what those goddamn bastards did to him!" I thought. I was only six, but it wasn't a six-year-old's thought. I felt like I wanted to kill somebody.

Crosses always bothered me after that. Later, in college, I studied the symbol's deeper meanings, along with the ennobling concepts of sacrifice, grace, forgiveness, the soul's triumph over death, and its eventual reunion with its immortal father. And while they're all comforting ideas, viscerally, the cross still reminds me of humanity at its worst, and of things gone horribly wrong.

The symbol had played a central role in three recurring nightmares, and I decided if it happened again, I would definitely talk with my mother. Maybe it was time for me to go see a doctor or something.

***

That day, Thursday December 2, flew by normally.

My father was leaving for Boston the next day for the big 76ers—Celtics showdown in The Garden. After dinner, I finished my homework, goofed around a little and finally went to bed. As usual, I put on the radio and listened for a while, but I never got sleepy. I was much too agitated.

I kept thinking about my social life, my schoolwork, and the upcoming game with the Celtics. But I knew that wasn't the real reason I couldn't fall asleep. I was just too afraid I was going to have that nightmare again, and I couldn't face the idea of going through it all one more time.

I don't remember getting tired or drifting off to sleep. I was just lying in my bed with my eyes closed and the very next thing I knew, I felt a funny sensation in my stomach, like I was in a moving car that had just come over a hill and was on its way down. I opened my eyes and saw my hands resting on the steering wheel of a car. I looked over them at the hood and realized I was driving my father's Cadillac.

I came down the hill on Spring Avenue and turned left onto Heather Road, as I had done a million times before. Our house was on the corner.

I noticed that there were a few cars parked in front as I drove by. I made a right turn into the driveway, pulled up, and got out of the car. I walked around to the back door and into the kitchen.

My mother was on the phone with her back to me. She didn't seem to notice that I had come in and didn't turn around. My Uncle Ray, my father's younger brother, was standing in front of the stove. He had his arms folded across his chest and was staring down at the floor. He didn't look up or acknowledge me at all. It was like I wasn't there.

I walked through the dining room, into the main hall, and up the stairs. I turned left at the top and walked down the hallway toward my sister's room. As always, her door was closed, but it was opened just a crack. I walked up to the door, put my right hand on it, and stopped for a moment. I stared at the back of my hand and thought, "Well, this is it."

I pushed the door open. Sybil was standing in the back of the room near her bed, with a few friends. She looked up at me.

"Daddy's dead," she said. "We don't have a daddy anymore."

"This is terrible," I thought to myself. "But why are you talking like this? You're twenty years old, and you sound like a four-year-old."

I didn't say anything and walked out of her room, down the hall, and into my room. I sat down on my bed, and suddenly got overwhelmed with an intense anger at God.

"Why did you have to do this?" I thought. "Why in the world did you have to do this?" I smashed my fist down on the large end table next to my bed.

As soon as my fist hit the table, everything changed, and I was startled to find that I wasn't sitting on my bed anymore - I was lying in it. In another moment, I realized I must have fallen asleep and the whole thing had been a nightmare. The room was gray with the first light of dawn. And according to my clock radio, it was a few minutes before six.

Of course, my first feeling was relief. I had just gone through a chillingly lifelike experience that had ended with my sister telling me that my father had died. And now, thank God, none of it was real. It had all been just a bad dream.

But in actuality, there had been nothing dreamlike

about it. In fact, it had been every bit as real as any experience I'd ever had in my life. I was happy about one thing, though – at least I hadn't had a repeat of that same nightmare with the killer and the cross, which was a plus. Luckily, that was over.

33

In Real Life

It was Friday morning, December 3, 1965. I picked up my good friend Marty and drove him to school, which I did on most school days. This time, though, as soon as he got in the car, I told him about my dream. I had a funny feeling I should tell someone. In case it came true, I didn't want to be the only one who knew about it in advance. It seemed like the kind of thing that could drive you nuts if you didn't handle it right.

We only talked about it for a few minutes as we drove, and then switched to our plans for the upcoming weekend, which was packed with social events. The school day flew by in a flash, and the next thing I knew, it was Friday night.

***

There was a big party and I was going to drive across town, pick up my girlfriend, and bring her with me. It was a half-hour ride each way, and when it came time to leave, suddenly I didn't feel like driving by myself. I called Marty and asked him to come with me. He agreed if we didn't take the Sprite, which was only a two-seater. He was six-one and didn't want to be cramped-in with a third person.

My mother was getting ready to watch the Celtics game on TV in the living room. My father was already up in Boston. I went in and asked if it was OK for me to take her car. "You better not," she replied. "Sybil has a bunch of friends coming over, and she may need it."

She turned on the TV and sat down on the couch. "Take the Caddy," she said, nonchalantly. Without giving it a second thought, I hopped into my father's car and picked up Marty.

About twenty minutes into the ride, I felt like hearing some music. "Let's listen to the radio," I said and turned it on. I hit the middle button, but there was no sound at all—dead silence, which was very strange. That button was always set to our local rock 'n roll station, and a loud-mouth deejay, a pop song, or an annoying commercial was blaring all the time. But now I heard absolutely nothing, and it was deafening. The silence lasted long enough that I thought the radio was broken.

Finally, an announcer in a solemn voice came on and said—"We have just received a report from the Boston Garden that the owner of the 76ers, Ike Richman, has collapsed at courtside." He paused. "His condition is unknown."

I quickly turned it off. I had never heard anyone speak like that on this station before, and I didn't want to hear any more. We drove to my girlfriend's house. As soon as we got there, I called home. My sister answered, and she sounded perky and happy, like she was having fun with her friends and everything was fine.

"Sybil, what's happening?" I asked.

"Oh, nothing," she replied lightly. "Everything's

fine. Listen, Mommy is leaving for New York soon, and she wants to see you before she goes. She's waiting for you, so come right home."

"Sure, I replied. "I'll be right back.

"Great," she said, cheerfully. Then in a slightly different tone, she added, "Come home now, David. Just come right home." It was a minor change, but I heard it in a major way.

"This could be anything," I said to Marty as we drove back. "It could be indigestion. Or maybe he fainted from the lack of air in the place." I paused, then said the obvious. "Or he could be dead."

I thought about it for a few seconds. Sybil had said everything was OK, but that didn't mean anything. What else would she say? I was sixteen, had only been driving for a few months, and had a long ride home on the expressway.

Oddly, looking back on it, the lucid dream I'd had the night before—the one that began with me driving my father's car—never occurred to me at all. I had completely forgotten about it.

I kept driving along and then got to Spring Avenue. I crested over the hill, and as I started driving down it, I got a funny feeling in my stomach. I looked at my hands resting on the steering wheel and gazed at the hood of my father's car.

That moment began one of the strangest experiences of my life. My dream from the previous night started to come true, in front of my startled eyes. As I lived through it, I knew exactly what was coming next, and it was uncanny. I turned left onto Heather Road and drove past the cars that were parked in front of the house, just like in the dream.

It felt sort of like a déjà vu, but very different. Déjà vu means "already seen," and you feel like somehow, you've already lived through the experience that you're currently having. It's like remembering the present. But it's usually pretty vague, and only lasts an instant.

There was nothing vague about the experience I was having. Quite the opposite. It was crystal clear. And it didn't vanish at all. It just went on and on.

As I drove along, one part of my mind was normal, with regular thoughts and feelings. But another part knew what was coming and wanted to change it. As I was about to turn into the driveway, that part said, "Park on the street. Don't turn into the driveway. You know what's coming if you park in the driveway. Don't do it. Do something else!"

That seemed logical and I decided to park on the street. But then I made a disturbing discovery: I had no control at all over what was happening. Even though I clearly decided to park on the street, I robotically turned into the driveway, shut off the engine and got out of the car.

"Don't go in the back door. Go around front," I told myself as I started walking. "Just go in the front door. Do not go around back. Don't do it!" I thought about whether I had the key to the front door with me, but I knew it didn't matter. It was like I was watching a movie that had already been shot, and now I was just living through it. And not only did I know what was coming, I also knew there was no changing it.

I got to the back door and walked into the kitchen. Sure enough, just like the dream, my mother was on the phone with her back to me and never noticed me. Neither did my Uncle Ray, who was standing in front of the stove with his arms folded across his chest, looking down at the floor.

As I walked out into the hall, I knew it was time to go upstairs and face the news. It didn't matter what I thought or did. What was coming was coming.

I got to the top of the stairs and looked down the hallway at the door to my sister's room. I could see that it was closed but opened just a crack. I walked over and put my right hand on the door. I looked at my hand and had the same thought I'd had in the dream. "Well, this is it."

I pushed the door open. My sister was in the exact spot near her bed, surrounded by friends. She looked up at me. "Daddy's dead. We don't have a daddy anymore."

And then I had the same thought that I had had in the dream. "This is terrible. But why are you talking like this? You're twenty years old, and you sound like a four-year-old."

Then, still without choice, I walked out into the hall and down to my room. I sat on my bed and became overwhelmed with the same intense anger at God.

"Why did you have to do this?" I thought in a rage of anger, confusion, and despair. "Why in the world did you have to do this?" And just like the dream, I smashed my fist down on the end table next to my bed. But in my dream, I woke up.

This time, when my fist hit the table, I was abruptly snapped back into normal reality again. Except there was no such thing as normal anymore. Instead of waking up from a nightmare that was only a dream, I started living a nightmare that was real. And the devastating truth was clear—this was no dream, this was real life. My father was dead.

34

Be Strong, Davy: Part 2

Quite simply, my family got hit by an atomic bomb and our whole world was destroyed. All we knew was that in the first quarter of the Celtics game, my father suffered a major heart attack and died at courtside. My mother had seen it on TV. Although she had spoken briefly to someone who was there, like everybody else, we really learned about it from the newspapers the next day.

He had been sitting next to the team bench, as he always did. Dolph Schayes sat on his left, and a reporter from the Christian Science Monitor was on his right.

It had been a brutal night for us from the beginning. The Garden was sold out. It was a typical 76ers—Celtics Battle Royale, and the packed crowd was intense, showering their heroes with adoration and spewing venom on us. If it had been in Philly, it would have been exactly the same thing, only the other way around.

Chet Walker had been fouled, and a time-out had been called. The score was tied 13–13, which was ironic because my father was extremely superstitious. The teams were walking back onto the court, and then suddenly, the reporter felt my father leaning heavily on him, gasping for air.

Dolph knew something was wrong and stood up. Red Auerbach looked over from the Boston bench. "Get a doctor!" Dolph shouted. "Quick! Get a doctor!"

Red grabbed the team's doctor, and they came running over to my father, who had already collapsed onto the floor, but they were too late. There was no sign of life left in him, and he was carried out on a stretcher. The doctor said he probably died before his body hit the floor.

When play resumed, the 76ers rattled off 14 unanswered points and went into the locker room at halftime hoping to get some good news. But instead, they got the worst. Ike was gone.

As soon as the second half started, they dominated every aspect of the game. Wilt was a madman, scoring 28 points, grabbing 30 rebounds, and blocking 9 shots. Luke, Wally, Chet, Hal, and Billy were all in double figures. They won by an unthinkable 16 points and blew the stunned Celtics out of The Garden. The dazed crowd was silent.

Back in the locker room, under normal circumstances, the atmosphere would have been exuberant, but of course, it was the opposite, and nobody even noticed the win. Dolph hadn't even watched the last five minutes of the game. He just sat on the bench with his head in his hands. Afterward, he was too grief-stricken to talk.

Wilt was completely devastated. One paper said that after the game, "the giant Philadelphia star sat in the club dressing room for fifteen minutes with his head buried into his arms." When he finally talked to reporters, he said, "I have known Ike ever since I was in high school. I can't look back on anything I have or anything I am that I don't owe to him. He was my friend and my advisor. But he was much more than a friend to me. Much more."

Our three major newspapers covered it fully. The

Daily News was kind enough to include a close-up shot of my father lying dead on the floor. It was hard to take. But like the rest of the strange world I found myself in, I just had to get used to it. One thing you learn fast from sudden death—what's done is done.

I got halfway through the papers and then just put them down. Suddenly, the exploits of the team were completely meaningless to me. I went downstairs to see my mother.

When I walked into the kitchen, it was the first time we were alone together. She was on the phone, in the middle of a million details, making funeral arrangements with the undertaker, talking to the caterer, and getting ready for the tidal wave that was about to descend upon us.

With the phone to her ear, she looked me straight in the eye and silently told me everything I needed to know. She was rock-solid, in complete control, and as bad as this was, we were going to get through it. Like a fighter pilot whose copilot had just been killed, suddenly she was flying solo, in serious turbulence, with flak everywhere. But the mission was still on. And the only thing to do was tighten your seatbelt and keep flying. She had guts of steel, knew exactly what she was up against, and most importantly, nothing was going to hurt her kids.

***

Later that Saturday evening, right after sundown, we went over to the funeral parlor to view my father's body. It was just our immediate family.

When we got there, I tried to get mentally prepared. Just a few months earlier, I had stood next to my father, looking at my Uncle George's dead body. Now I would be looking at him. Uncle George was like a pasty wax figure.

230

I couldn't imagine how bad my father was going to be. As we approached the plain, brown coffin. I got ready for the worst. But when I looked in, I wasn't at all prepared for what I saw.

He looked fantastic, and he seemed completely alive. His eyes were closed, but he didn't look dead. In fact, he didn't even look asleep. He had an animated expression on his face that I had seen a million times, like he had just gotten a great idea. He seemed ready to sit up and tell us about it. And he was sure we were going to love it. I couldn't stop staring at him. It was unsettling. He just looked too good.

Maybe it was because he had died suddenly and hadn't been sick. Or maybe it was because he'd been dead for less than a day. Or maybe the mortician was a genius with hair, makeup, and lighting. Probably all of the above. Whatever it was, it was a real shock. The only way you could tell he was dead was that he wasn't breathing.

***

I was fine until we got home, and I walked into the kitchen. I looked at our table with the four chairs spread around it, in their usual positions; and I totally lost it. I ran into the hall closet and cried into the coats for a few minutes. Then I regained my composure and came back out.

That started happening to me a lot. I always wanted to be alone whenever I felt like crying, which was often. There was something deeply personal about it, and I needed to shut off the outside world. This was just between me and myself.

When we got back from the funeral home, a few people had gathered at the house. It was quiet and private, with only some immediate relatives and close friends.

When I walked into the entrance hall, I was surprised to see Wilt sitting there. He was all alone, slumped over in one of the chairs, with his head in his hands. I couldn't handle the sight of him. It brought the whole thing home in a way I wasn't ready for. I ran into the bathroom and cried my eyes out for a few minutes. I'm pretty sure he never saw me.

About ten minutes later, we saw each other in the hall and again, I couldn't take it. I turned, went into my parents' room and closed the door.

When I came out and started walking down the hall, I could see him standing by himself, staring into my father's office where the two of them had spent so much time together. I turned around to walk back to my parents' room. I didn't think he had seen me, and I was sure that I was out of his reach. But, somehow, he stretched out his long right arm and wrapped his hand around my shoulder. As soon as he touched me, I broke up. He pulled me close and held me firmly against his side. I collapsed into him and started crying hard.

He put his forearm against the wall, high above the doorway to the office, up near the ceiling, and buried his face in it. I could feel his body shaking with sobs as we stood there together. Then, from all the way up there, I heard his deep voice say, "Be strong, Davy. It's time to be strong."

35 — Just One Rose

Sunday, December 5, 1965, was my father's funeral, which was held at Temple Sholom. For months, we had been focused on three big events, scheduled one Sunday after the next: the Bond dinner, the engagement party, and my mother's fiftieth. Now it turned out there was a fourth— his funeral. Of course, it wasn't on anyone's calendar. But nevertheless, here it was.

It started out with a private viewing for family and friends in the synagogue lobby. It's against the religion to put an opened coffin inside the sanctuary, so the viewing was held out there. It was a bright day and the lobby was filled with sunlight. As I looked at him, he still had that same animated expression on his face. But it was a day later, and he was a day deader.

It was a rough hour. As we stood next to the coffin, our family and close friends lined up to say goodbye. I watched as all the people I had known all my life, every single one of them, broke down in shock and grief at the sight of him. His aunts and uncles from the old country were crying and screaming in Yiddish, and two of them fainted. It was terribly painful. By the end of the hour, it was already the worst day of my life, and it hadn't even started yet.

Finally, they closed the coffin and opened the

sanctuary doors. They wheeled it into the synagogue and we followed behind.

***

To my surprise, it was packed with mourners. We had been shut off and hadn't heard them come in. All the seats were taken and there was no place left to stand. According to the papers, about twenty-five hundred people surrounded the building outside as well. Maybe they had come to pay their respects, or maybe just to see the team.

They had all walked in together and stood against one wall as a group. Wilt was in the middle, but he wasn't Wilt Chamberlain anymore. He was just another heartbroken soul, who had come to say goodbye to his dear old friend, really his second father.

There was such an outpouring of grief, it took a while to get the place quieted down. Sudden death is a real killer. It adds shock to the sorrow, driving home the truth that no matter who you are, the end can come at any time.

It was all very personal. The cantor, who my father's committee had hired ten years earlier, started singing the opening prayer and when he got to the word that meant "compassion," he burst into tears. After he finally finished, the rabbi began the service with a portion from the 24th Psalm of David. He had been close with my father for over twenty years and felt it was especially appropriate.

"Who shall ascend the mountain of the Lord? And who shall stand in his holy place?" he read. "He that hath clean hands and a pure heart, who hath not lifted his soul up to vanity, nor sworn deceitfully. He shall receive the blessing from the Lord. And righteousness from the God of his salvation."

He choked up at that point and had to stop. Then he composed himself, cleared his throat and went on. He eventually began the eulogy. Toward the end of it he said, "Just three weeks ago today, we all gathered together to honor Ike at the Israeli Bonds dinner held in the auditorium of this very building. It was a warm and wonderful event. And at the end, I watched Clare and Ike stand at the door and say good-night to everyone."

"We all thought we were just saying good-night to him," he teared up again. "But only God knew that we were really saying goodbye. Goodbye and farewell. How perfect it was that we all got to be together one last time before his Father called him home."

After the service, we drove to the cemetery. The police closed the center section of Roosevelt Boulevard and a few squad cars led the way.

At the cemetery, the coffin was placed on a metal stand, over the open grave. The rabbi said a few prayers and then it was time for us to say the Mourner's Kaddish. When the first word came out of my mouth, I remembered that only eight days earlier, I had been sitting with my father in synagogue and he had made me promise that I would do this for him after he died. I had completely forgotten about it.

After we finished, the rabbi took a small spade, reached into a container of dirt, and put a pile of it on the coffin. "What are you doing?" I thought. "Don't do that. You're going to get it dirty."

And then, it all really hit me. Until then, the whole thing had been like a show. My father was immaculately dressed and perfectly groomed, lying in this beautiful wooden box that was now resting on a shiny silver stand. They had bright-green artificial turf spread all around, so you didn't see any dirt or the other graves. It was all so clean.

But now, the show was over, and it was time to get down to the real business at hand. They were going to take this pretty box with him in it, and bury it deep in the ground, under six feet of dirt. And that would be that.

For the first time, I fully understood that he was really gone, and I was never going to see him again. Never again hear his voice, listen to his wisdom and counsel, hear him laugh or sense the nobility of his spirit. And I would never again feel his love and protection. Our time together was over. We had reached the end.

***

When we got back to the house, my mother and I were walking arm in arm from the driveway to the back door. As we passed the rose garden, she stopped dead in her tracks and gasped. All the rose bushes were bare except for one in the middle, which had a big saffron-orange rose on it, in full bloom.

It was early December, and she was sure that when we'd left, just a few hours before, there hadn't even been a bud there. She got a pair of scissors, cut the rose off, put it in a vase of water and kept it next to her bed. It stayed colorful, bright, and alive, and she took a deep inhale of its sweet fragrance every night before she went to sleep.

That was the beginning of what is called "Sitting Shiva," which went from that Sunday afternoon until the following Friday at sundown. My grandparents moved into our house, and we had services there twice a day.

It's a somber period where you leave your normal life in the outside world behind. All the mirrors are covered up with sheets, and you're not allowed to watch TV or listen to the radio, not that I ever wanted to.

Just about every person I had ever known came to visit us. Everyone was unbelievably caring and kind. My mother said several times, that even though it had been so painful, in its own way, every part of it had been beautiful.

***

Finally, it was Friday afternoon and the shiva period was about to end. We would have dinner and then go to synagogue. It was the first time we would leave the house in almost a week. In the late afternoon, I went into my father's office to spend some time alone there. When I sat down at his desk, I noticed a small pile of cards set aside from all the others, with a paperweight on it.

We had received a huge number of condolence cards. A lot of them were contributions to charities in his honor, and my mother had separated them into different piles, so she could write thank-you notes in response.

This one pile caught my eye. It only had about ten cards in it and was clearly separated from the rest. I started looking through them. The first one was a regular sympathy card, but in the blank space on the left were three large hand-drawn, swastikas. Underneath, someone had written, "One more dead Jew—The world is a cleaner place!"

I picked up the next one. Again, it was a normal condolence card, but inside was a big, hand-drawn cross dripping with blood with fire below it, and the words, "Burn in Hell, Nigger-Loving Jew." I flipped through the rest of them; they were all similar.

One of my father's partners and a close family friend, Jimmy Price, was the commissioner of the township's police department and had been expecting this kind of thing. He told my mother to let him see any hate mail that came. He was close with the FBI, and if needed, they would act appropriately. There was only a small amount of crank mail from different parts of the country. None of it was local, so he wasn't concerned.

A few hours later, at sundown, the shiva officially ended. The house was empty now except for my mother, my brother and his wife, my sister, and me. When it was time, my mother called us into the dining room for dinner.

I was a little surprised. I thought we'd just be eating in the kitchen. But it was Friday night, and my mother had set the dining room up for our usual Shabbat dinner. Everything was the same as always, with my father's chair at the head and his place set for him. We all stood there a little awkwardly. It was almost like she had set his place in his honor, and we didn't quite know what to do.

My mother looked at my brother and motioned for him to sit down in my father's seat. Mike went over and stood there for a second, then sat down. As soon as he did, he burst into tears.

My mother looked at him compassionately and waited a few seconds. Then with a soft, empathetic tone she said resolutely, "Get used to it."

And he did. We all did. There was no choice. We said the prayers, ate our dinner, and then left for synagogue. Shiva was over.

36

Not This Year

It was time for me to begin the slow, inch-by-inch journey from catastrophe back to normal. But normal was a long way off. I went to school Monday morning and walked back into my everyday life. Everyone was extremely kind, and I had a ton of school work to catch up with, which helped divert my attention. But I was totally shell-shocked.

As the routine of everyday life set back in, amazingly, everything was the same as it had been before my father died—same people, same school, same schedule, same life; it was all exactly the same. Except nothing was the same. And it never would be again.

I played it brave, but the center of my world had been destroyed, and there was now a gaping chasm of grief in its place. I had to learn to walk around it, but I still fell into it several times a day, and it broke me apart every time.

Finally, after about a month, a few small things slowly started bringing me back to life. It began when my brother's first child, was born. It was a boy and of course, they named him Isaac.

I came to visit the day they brought him home from the hospital. He was sound asleep, but they let me go in the room as long as I didn't disturb him. I walked over to the crib and put my hand on it. He was just a few days old and I had never seen a baby that young before. His brand-new, innocent face was unmarked by any traces of emotion or thought. It was hard to believe that we all start out this way, and the innocence of it moved me.

As I stood there with my hand on his crib, it felt oddly familiar, and I soon realized that I had been in the same position at my father's funeral, just six weeks earlier. Only then, I was standing next to a coffin, looking at death. Now, I was standing next to a crib, looking at birth – the sadness of the end of one life, followed by the joy of the beginning of another.

For the first time, I got a real sense of the beauty of the cycle of life. The triumphs and tragedies, the beginnings and endings were like a wheel—one following another. As I looked at the purity of the newborn's face, I got a feeling of continuity that helped soften the blow of finality.

Still, I felt sad that the new baby and his grandfather would never know each other. Then I remembered that my father had told me he would never be the grandfather to this child. It had only been a few months earlier, but it hadn't occurred to me until then. His comment had sounded so strange back then. Now it was just one more prophetic piece of the mysterious puzzle surrounding my father's death.

***

A few weeks later, my aunt called my mother with a problem. Hommie was my father's younger sister. All her life, he had been her protector and confidant, and his sudden death had devastated her. She was also my mother's best friend. After my parents' marriage, they had moved into my father's parent's house above the store with the rest of the family, and they had become as close as sisters.

She said that several months earlier, she had given my father some money to hold for her—about $4,000—and was wondering if my mother knew anything about it. My mother had no idea. My father had never mentioned it to her and it wasn't in any of the papers he had left behind. Now, $4,000 was a fair amount of money back then, so it was kind of serious. Regardless, they promised each other they would not let it become an issue between them.

My mother said she would start looking into it immediately and see what she could find. The first thing the next morning, she went into my father's office to go through his papers again. As soon as she walked in, she noticed one book that was sticking out from all the others on a bookshelf, clearly separated from the rest. She went right to it, opened it up, and a paper fell out onto the floor.

To her amazement, written in my father's handwriting, it was an exact accounting of Hommie's money, with all the details—the amount, what bank it was in, and the account number. My mother was certain the book had not been there when she left the office, just the night before.

She called Hommie. They had a good, long cry and happily resolved the situation. The whole thing did them both a lot of good. In fact, it did us all a lot of good.

***

Finally, two months later, something profound

happened with my grandfather. It was Passover and my mother had both Seders at our house, as always. The first one was April 5, 1966, exactly four months to the day after my father's funeral.

Our family was closer than ever. Not only had we all gone through the death trauma together, we had also closed ranks around my father's parents, who were still struggling. Supposedly, nothing is worse than the death of one's child, and losing my father had clearly drained the life out of them. They were both completely devastated.

About forty people came. Passover is a happy, festive holiday and we all behaved like everything was normal. Nobody even mentioned my father whose absence was the eight-hundred-pound gorilla in the room everyone was ignoring.

We all sat down for the Seder. My grandfather's seat was in the center of the head table. The service starts with three blessings. He stood up and cleared his throat. We all joined him as he sang the first one, over the wine, and then the one over the bread. We all said, "Amen," and waited for him to begin the third one, called the Shehecheyanu.

It's a particularly momentous two-thousand-year-old prayer, said only on certain special religious holidays. Simply translated, it means, "Blessed art thou, o Lord our God, who has given us life, sustained us and brought us to this great day."

It is sometimes invoked on non-religious occasions as well. For instance, at the stroke of midnight on May 14, 1948, when the State of Israel gained its independence, the Government's first official act was to recite the Shehecheyanu.

As Zayde stood there getting ready to sing it, something seemed to be bothering him. He began, but his voice was shaky and weak. When he got to the actual word Shehecheyanu, he choked up and couldn't go on. He just stood there for a moment, then sat down, burst into tears, and buried his head in his hands.

He obviously had been holding back his feelings all night, but when he got to that word the damn broke, and the pain in his heart came flooding out through his tears. He was crying from the depths of his soul and it was one of the saddest things I'd ever seen.

My Uncle Ray, his youngest child, came over to him and put his arm around his shoulder. "OK, Pop, it's OK. Come on, let's do the prayer together. We'll all do it with you. Come on."

"No," Zayde responded, with his head still buried in his hands. We waited another minute for him to regain his composure. He finally stopped crying, but he didn't budge. He just sat there, crumpled over.

"Pop, we have to do the prayer," Uncle Ray said. "We can't go on without it. You just have to do it. Now, come on. We'll all do it together."

Zayde finally sat up and wiped his eyes with his napkin. "No," he said, recomposed, but firm. "No. Not this year."

He turned the page of the book and cleared his throat. My uncle stood there, but after a moment went back to his seat. Zayde continued the Seder and we all turned our pages and followed along. There was nothing else to do.

But as he sang, a noticeable change came over him. His old confidence seemed to be coming back and his voice got stronger with each prayer. Everyone noticed it and soon, the whole room was elevated. And as he kept going, he kept getting stronger.

It wasn't like he had been miraculously healed and the pain had gone away. No, the pain was still clearly there. But now he seemed to be on top of it instead of under it, and that was a huge difference. I could see the light returning to his pale-blue eyes. They had been vacant for so long, I had forgotten the sparkle they used to have.

I've often wondered what happened to him that night. We never discussed it, but I knew that in my grandfather's world, the world of the true cantor, when you prayed, you prayed from the heart. You meant it. And he couldn't sing that prayer for real. He just couldn't thank God for keeping us alive, when his son had been ripped away from him, only a few months earlier. So, he refused to follow the form and instead of faking it, he just moved on.

At first, I thought it might have been a statement of doubt or anger, but it didn't look that way. He had just hit a personal impasse and had gone around it. And as he did, his spirit kept strengthening.

Could the sincerity in his heart have created an inner bridge that had brought him closer to God? Had he gotten to the essence of the prayer by refusing to follow the form? Who knows? According to the mystics, there are profound inner experiences that transcend rites and rituals. Well, he certainly was a mystic. And without a doubt, something profound had happened to him.

So, three small, but significant events – my experience with the birth of the baby, the resolution of Aunt Hommie's money, and my grandfather's transformation, each had a deeply positive effect on me and opened my eyes to more light. But they were nothing compared to what was coming next.

37

Give Me Back the Ring

The 1966 NBA semifinals began around that time. I had gotten back into the 76ers and had gone to some games, but obviously, it wasn't the same. In the face of life and death, who really cares about winning and losing? We got to the Eastern finals and the Celtics blew us out. In reality, I was glad it was over. Following the team just made everything worse, like constantly reopening a wound.

Of course, I was saying Kaddish, keeping the promise I had made to my father. We joined the synagogue near our house, and my brother and I went there every morning and night, seven days a week.

From the beginning, we got very close to the rabbi, who took us under his wing. He was one of the most enlightened, caring, and charismatic people I had ever met, and he taught as powerfully as he prayed. He was also a genuinely happy person which meant a lot because, in his pastoral work, he was well acquainted with all the sufferings life presents. It was always uplifting to be in his company and sphere of influence.

We became part of the small community of daily worshipers and it was a big help. The stability of it, being with other mourners, and having daily exposure to the power of the rabbi, kept a firm structure around us, like a cast on a broken bone.

I could see that even though Kaddish is said to honor the dead, it's a great help to the living, lighting their path as they make their way back to full life. Maybe that's why my father was so insistent about it; he knew how much it would help me. You never know.

Around mid-May, my brother had to get ready to take the bar exam. There was a three-part prep course, but it was only held at night, which meant he would have to miss services. He was unhappy about it, but there was nothing he could do.

So, the first night of the course became the first time he didn't make it to synagogue. I went without him, came home as usual, did my homework, and eventually went to bed. I have no recollection of getting tired or falling asleep. I was just lying there, and the next thing I knew, I found myself back in the chapel of the synagogue once again. I started reliving the same exact events that had just happened a few hours earlier. It was like an instant replay, but instead of watching it, I was reliving it.

Just like before, services ended, and I walked out of the chapel. But this time, when I entered the main lobby, I heard a sharp sound. "Psst! Psst!" It came from my left. I looked over at the dark corner near the sanctuary doors and suddenly, my father stepped out of the shadows.

Amazed, I walked right over to him. As I got closer, he gave me a warm smile and I was struck by how great he looked. He was wearing a gray suit with a purple shirt. The collar was opened, and he had a dark, healthy suntan like he had been in the Caribbean or Hawaii for a few months. He also seemed a little younger, with slightly more hair, which was slicked back. In short, he looked tremendous.

246

"Where's Michael?" he asked, as soon as I got close.

"Oh, he couldn't come tonight," I said. "He has to study for the bar exam. They're having a cram course, and tonight's the first class."

"Oh, right, right. That's good," he said, sounding like he knew exactly what I was talking about. "He'll pass it. He'll do fine. He's going to become a lawyer, and he'll go right into the practice. Everything's going to work out well for him." Then he got a little serious. "But, watch out for your sister, though," he said soberly. "She's not doing so great."

"Sybil?" I wondered. "What's the matter with Sybil?"

I didn't say anything, but as I thought about it, I remembered that she had never shown any emotion after he died. She had been extremely stoic, always stone-faced, never crying or even shedding a tear. Maybe that had something to do with whatever it was he was talking about.

"Oh yeah," I said. "She didn't show any emotion after you d—" I was just about to say the word "died," when the reality of what was happening hit me like a ton of bricks. Suddenly I remembered the truth of the matter — that he was, in fact, dead. I guess I had been so glad to see him, I hadn't realized it at first. But now it all came rushing came back into me, full blast.

The reason I hadn't seen him for all this time wasn't that he had been away on a tropical island. It was because he had dropped dead on the floor of the Boston Garden six months earlier. He was long since dead and buried, and yet here he was, standing in the synagogue lobby, talking to me like everything was normal.

"Wait a minute, wait a minute," I exclaimed. "What are you doing here? You're dead!"

"No," he said, with a slight chuckle. "No, no. That wasn't real."

"What?" I asked.

"It was just a trick," he replied. "It wasn't real."

"What do you mean, it wasn't real?" I shot back, a little perturbed. "Of course, it was real!" How could he say it wasn't real? It was the worst thing that had ever happened to me. Everything about it was a nightmare. Our family was completely devastated, and since then, we had gone through month after month of relentless pain. I wished to God it wasn't real, but unfortunately, it was as real as it gets.

"You died. You're dead," I blurted out, even more upset. "It was terrible. There was this big funeral, and everyone was hysterical. It was awful" A wave of raw pain welled up inside of me. "It was horrible. You died! We buried you and you're dead!"

I was ready to break down in tears. But then, just like old times, he made his familiar gesture and held up his right hand, signaling me to calm down and listen to him. Just seeing him do it made me feel a little better.

"It wasn't real," he said, calmly. "It was just a trick."

"What are you talking about?" I asked, bewildered.

"A trick. You know—a stunt, a gimmick."

I still had no idea what he meant but I didn't say anything.

"Listen to me," he said, sympathetically. "There is no death. It's just a public-relations stunt God does to get people to think about him. That's all it is. It's not real."

I didn't know what to say. There was absolutely, positively no question about the fact that he had died. It was irrefutable. And yet here he was—alive and well, happy and healthy, telling me it was all just a stunt. As confident as ever, he certainly looked like he knew what he was talking about. He looked great. In fact, I'd never seen him look better.

"See?" he said, with a smile. "It's all just a trick." Then he added, "Some trick!"

At that point, my mind went blank. I don't think I could think anymore, and frankly, I didn't care. It was just such a relief to be with him again and listen to him explain something to me. It didn't matter if I understood it or not.

As I looked at him, I realized I had forgotten how much I really missed him. I hadn't seen him for six months. It had been an eternity of constant pain and I had gotten used to it. But now, alive or dead, we were back together again, and the pain was gone. I was happy and felt like my old self—two long-lost and long-forgotten feelings.

"I see you're wearing my ring," he said, looking down at my right hand. He used to wear a black star sapphire pinky ring that he got when he went to the Japan Olympics to sign Luke Jackson. My mother gave it to me after he died, and I wore it every day.

"Listen," he said somewhat soberly. "The stone in that ring has a vibration that's bad for your body. I don't want you to wear it anymore." I didn't say anything.

Then his face lit up. "Hey! I've got an idea," he said. "Since I never really died, why don't you give it back to me?"

Without giving it a second thought, I took the ring off and held it up between the thumb and forefinger of my right hand. He reached up and held it exactly the same way. I thought he was going to take it, but he didn't. Instead, we both stood there, holding the ring between us, like a statue.

After a moment, I felt it start to vibrate. Then, like an instrument being tuned to a higher note, something within me quickened. The ring began to glow, getting brighter by degrees until eventually, the whole room was filled with a brilliant light.

But it was more than just a light. I could sense a presence to it, a beauty that was extremely comforting. And it felt familiar to me as well, like I knew it from somewhere—another time and place from long before my memory began.

I felt myself being slowly pulled into it, as though it had its own field of gravity. It got stronger, like the current of a river nearing the ocean, and the light got even brighter. The more light I saw, the lighter I felt, along with a deep sense of happiness and joy. It was intoxicating. And finally, an all-encompassing love enveloped me, and I lost contact with space and time.

I have no idea how long it lasted, but I finally began to regain awareness of my body. There was a gentle transition, almost like the physical world gelled into reality around me and I realized I was lying in my bed, wearing my pajamas. It took a little more time, but I realized it had all been just a dream.

Soon, I was completely back in the real world. Obviously, my life was unchanged, and my father was still dead. Naturally, I was disappointed. As fulfilling as the experience had been, the whole thing was just a fantasy my mind had created in my sleep.

Even so, it had been a deeply wonderful experience to feel happy again. It was the first time since the night he died, that the heavy burden I felt had been lifted from my heart. For those few moments, I had gotten to be my old self again. I had completely forgotten the way life used to be, before my road had turned, and I had come upon the Vale of Tears.

***

I began my day as usual. As I drove to school, I reflected on the dream from a psychological perspective. My second semester of psychology was almost over, and the mysterious workings of the mind were really starting to fascinate me.

As I thought about it, I was quite impressed by this dream. It had been a perfect mental placebo for me. In the theater of my mind, my father looked great. Healthy and smiling, he said he had never really died, and that it was only a PR stunt. He called it a gimmick, which I loved. It was a term he used a lot in the early days of the team, but I had forgotten all about it. Still, it was exactly the way he used to talk. Indeed, everything about him was familiar, comforting and reassuring, just the way I would want it to be.

And there was also this God theme running through it, which made perfect sense because I was getting so much religious exposure every day. In the dream, I had seen this beautiful light, filled with an essence of peace, happiness, and contentment. I felt like I was finally coming back home, experienced an overwhelming love, and then merged into it. All classic heaven stuff.

I didn't know what to make out of my father's ring though. I had given it back to him and it turned into light, which started the whole heaven part. I figured it probably had a subconscious meaning and I'd bring it up with my psychology teacher.

Anyway, as far as dreams go, it had been a real beauty. And if my mind's purpose was to comfort me and bring me a little happiness and peace, it had certainly done its job. I felt great in the dream. And as a matter of fact, I was still feeling pretty good as I drove along.

When I got to the school parking lot, I took the ring off and looked at it. I liked it, but I always felt a little odd wearing it. I had just turned seventeen, and it was the type of thing you'd see on a fifty-year-old man.

I didn't care, though. It was his, and I was going to wear it for the rest of my life and give it to my kids. I put it back on and went into school.

***

It was a Friday morning, and I had gym first period. When I got to my locker, I followed my usual routine. I wore two rings, a gold initial ring, and his black star sapphire. I took them both off and put them carefully inside my wallet, next to a ten-dollar bill I had. I was going to buy a new basketball after school.

I took off my wristwatch, wrapped it around my wallet, and put the whole thing in one of my shoes. Then, I put my books on top of my shoes and locked my locker. I double-checked the door and the lock to make sure it was all secure and tight as a drum. I had been doing the same thing twice a week for five years.

It was a beautiful May morning, and I played touch football with my friends, a bunch of jovial, eleventh-grade jocks. I took a shower and got dried off. Then, I opened my combination lock, swung open my locker door, and put my clothes on. I took the books off the top of my shoes, took out my wallet, removed my watch, and put it on my wrist. Then I opened my wallet to put on my rings - and the world stopped.

To my extreme shock and disbelief, my father's ring was gone!

Everything else was exactly as I had left it. My gold initial ring and the ten-dollar bill were still there, undisturbed. But his black star sapphire ring, the one I had given him in the dream just a few hours earlier, had disappeared without a trace.

Suddenly, reality didn't make any sense. What had just happened, quite simply could not have happened. It just wasn't possible. My head started spinning and I felt disoriented. I sat down on the bench in front of my locker and tried to pull myself together. To make sure I wasn't losing my mind, I went over all the details again to see if I had made a mistake. But I hadn't. I remembered everything precisely.

"Somebody must have stolen it," I thought for a second, but obviously, that didn't make any sense. The locker had been clearly undisturbed when I came back after my shower. The combination lock was still locked, and the door was untouched. And besides, why would someone steal just that one ring and leave the wallet, the watch, and the gold ring, not to mention the ten-dollar bill?

I thought about the dream again. It was now nine in the morning and I had only been awake for a couple of hours, so everything was still completely fresh in my mind. I realized how strange it had been. I didn't remember feeling drowsy or falling asleep and all of a sudden, I was back in the chapel. And there had been absolutely nothing dreamlike about it at all - I had never felt more awake in my life. On top of that, unlike my usual dreams, it hadn't faded a bit. Normally, I forget my dreams before I even start breakfast. But this time, I could remember every detail, especially my father's tan, smiling face.

He said that he hadn't really died and that it was a trick. Then he had me give him back his ring. When we held it, it turned into a brilliant light. And now, a few hours later, in real life, it had vanished into thin air. It just wasn't possible.

Still dazed, I sat in front of my locker for a few more

minutes and then the bell rang. I knew I had to hustle because my next class was all the way on the other side of school. There was nothing left to do but get on with my day. My logic had hit a brick wall.

I got up and started walking. But as I hurried along, I noticed that everything felt a little lighter, like the old bounce was coming back into my step.

38

What Becomes of the Brokenhearted

About two weeks later, I decided to run for school president. It took a lot of effort and focus, but everything fell into place and the election went my way. Naturally, my mother was happy and proud, and we both knew what it would have meant to my father. Of course, his absence made it all bittersweet. But it was more sweet than bitter, and that was a real first for me. As Poet Robert Frost had said in his old age, "In three words, I can sum up everything I've learned about life: It goes on." It does, and it did.

I seemed to be finding my stride once again. And the summer was just over the horizon. When it came, I had a great time at the shore, working at the same day camp with many of the same friends. And before I knew it, I was back in Elkins Park and the school year was about to begin.

So was the historic 1966–1967 NBA season, which would come to be known as the Season of the 76ers. With Wilt in the middle, surrounded by a cast of all-stars, our guys would totally dominate the league, rewrite the record books, and finally win the title. We were in for quite a ride.

***

As soon as senior year began, I loved every minute of it. In my term as president, I assumed a new level of responsibility and was busy with important projects every day. And, my emotional wounds had healed enough that I was fully engaged with the team again.

This was going to be our year, and everybody felt it. The season began on October 15, 1966, and we hit the ground running. Or to be more accurate, we demolished the league like lightning shattering an old barn. We won the first game by 16 points, the second by 9, the third by 29, and the fourth by 20.

Wilt couldn't be contained, and he was doing unheard-of things. In the second game, he tapped in a jump ball from the foul line. A few games later, he threw a length of the court, behind-the-back pass to Billy Cunningham, hitting him perfectly in stride as he broke toward the basket for a lay-up. We got a new coach, Alex Hannum. But other than that, this was the "dream team" my father had built, and every game was a sold-out, hometown celebration.

But the fifth game of the season was going to be the first true test of our strength. On Saturday night, October 29, 1966, the Celtics were coming to town. It would be the first time we'd face them since they'd humiliated us in the playoffs and it was going to be a major showdown. We were all optimistic, but with Boston, you never know. They were smart, talented, and tough. And a lot of times, according to Wilt, they were just plain lucky.

I was excited and couldn't wait for the game, but I also had a personal reason. I had a big date coming up that night. I had developed a serious crush on a certain girl at school and had finally gotten up enough nerve to ask her out. The game was going to be our first date.

About a month earlier, we had started noticing each other in the hall every morning, after second period. Our eyes would meet, but neither of us ever said a word. Still, the attraction was there and getting stronger. Before I knew it, I was falling really hard, and our daily eye-to-eye encounter quickly became the high point of my day.

Drop-dead gorgeous is a phrase that gets used a lot, but this girl really was. At least I felt like I was going to drop dead every time I saw her.

I put out some feelers and got the lowdown on her. Her name was Sally, and the word was, there was a lot more to her than just her looks. She was a singer and an actress in the school plays, and supposedly, she was really smart, with some depth to her. And she was funny, too. So, for me, she had all three of the major bases covered: pretty face, great body, and decent personality. Like most of the boys my age, I wasn't running all that deep at the time.

One day, as we looked each other in the eye for the millionth time, I simply said, "Hi."

"Hi," she said right back to me, but with a funny look on her face, like "My God, what took you so long?"

The following Saturday night, we were both at the first football dance of the year. We would catch each other's eyes across the room, but I just couldn't get up enough guts to approach her. Finally, the deejay announced the last slow dance of the night and put on, "What Becomes of the Brokenhearted." I knew it was now or never, so I walked up to her and asked her if she wanted to dance.

Standing under a fragrant halo of Shalimar perfume, she just smiled and nodded. When we embraced for the dance, it was like two poles of a magnet joining together, true teenager-in-love magical attraction. The song went on forever but ended much too soon. As it finished, I decided to ask her out for a date. I told her about the big upcoming Celtics game and asked if she'd like to come with me.

"OK!" she said with a smile. Even though I knew

she meant she was accepting my invitation, she sounded more like she was congratulating me for finally finding the courage to ask her out.

***

Two nights later, October 24, marked a major milestone for me. I said Kaddish for the final time, fulfilling the promise I had made to my father and the eleven-months of mourning came to an end. It had been a dark and trying period. But it was over now, and according to the practices of the religion, it was time for me to return fully to life. My date with Sally to the game would be my first Saturday night that wouldn't begin with me saying the Mourner's Kaddish. Somehow, it all seemed to fit together.

Even though my crush was in full swing, besides that one dance, I had never spent any time with her. I had no idea how it was going to go, so I decided if we beat the Celtics, it would be a good sign. I was always big on signs.

Saturday night finally came and once the game started, it was clear we were in for a dogfight. Every play was unbelievably intense, and the first quarter ended dead even, with a 27–27 tie. But then, as soon as the second quarter started, we quickly broke it wide opened, outscoring them by 11. We outscored them by 16 more in the third and another 15 in the fourth. The final score was almost ridiculous: 138–96. We slaughtered them. And not only did we win by 42 points, we held them to under 100 to boot. It seemed like a sure sign of things to come.

After the game, Sally and I went out to a local Italian restaurant with the team. As soon as we walked in, Wilt had us sit next to him. Whenever I had seen him since my father died, he was always especially attentive to me.

But this time, there was a little something extra. He had a twinkle in his eye every time he looked at me. And he would talk to Sally and then nudge me under the table—enthusiastically.

We had been on a double-date, and at one point, the other couple left in a different car. Now, on the upcoming ride home, Sally and I would be alone together for the first time. I was a little nervous. It was a half-hour ride back to Elkins Park, and I hoped it was going to work out alright. What if we ended up having nothing to say to each other? You never know.

Instead, the ride went by in a flash and we were on her street before we knew it. We both decided to keep driving around for a while and three more hours went by in another flash. By the time I finally got her home, we were both head over heels in love.

One afternoon the next week, I took her to my house after school. My mother and sister were in the kitchen when we walked in. My mother took one look at her and sent me upstairs on an errand, leaving the three of them alone together.

It was only a few minutes, but when I came back, they looked like they had known each other for years. My sister was smiling, and my mother had a glow on her face I had never seen before. And somewhere on some deep inner level that's still beyond me, I knew that the deal had been done.

And it had been. The two high-school sweethearts went on to become husband and wife, and eventually, father and mother. And the next thing we knew, along with our fair share of triumphs and tragedies, fifty years had flown by.

39

The Ball Belongs to Clare

Things took a magical turn after the big Celtics win, and the 76ers began to tear up the league. We won 10 of the next 11 games, by an average of 13 points per game. Sally and I were together all the time and went to every weekend home game, which would usually turn into a wild celebration. We would often join Wilt and the team at a restaurant near Convention Hall afterward. We were having the time of our lives.

I still made it a priority to visit my grandparents once a week. Bit by bit, they were coming back to life and it was especially clear with my grandfather. It was less than a year since my father had died, and he was still, obviously mourning the loss, but he was much more of his old self again. Maybe what happened to him at the Seder was part of it.

During one visit, we started talking about my sister. She had tumbled down a few steps in a classroom building. She wasn't hurt, but for a few moments, she just sat there, laughing. The trouble was, she couldn't stop. After a while, she went to see the nurse, who was concerned and admitted her to Temple Hospital for observation.

Sybil laughed all night, hardly sleeping. And then the next morning, she burst into tears, couldn't stop crying and was hysterical for hours. Then suddenly, the whole thing stopped, and she was herself again. She was back in class the next day.

"In that one dream, didn't your father tell you to watch out for her, that she wasn't doing well?" my grandfather asked me. He was right. She had never shown any emotions after my father died, and maybe this was how her grief finally got released, which made sense. Sybil always had her own way of doing everything.

I wasn't surprised that my grandfather had brought up the dream. He was always interested in the unusual things that had happened to me around the time of my father's death. And I always liked talking to him about them, because he was the only person who really believed me.

I'm pretty sure everyone else thought I had lost my marbles. I couldn't blame them. It had been a lot for an unprepared sixteen-year-old to handle and my mother had me talk to the rabbi and some teachers. In their rational explanations, the seemingly prophetic events never happened. To them, they were just false memories I had created to make myself feel better. But I knew what I had experienced, and no matter what anybody says, you know what you know.

That was one of my grandfather's favorite sayings – you know what you know. He was always big on keeping knowledge and beliefs separate. You had to know what you know, know what you only believe, and know the difference. Still, for him, dreams were in a special category, and could be bridges between worlds.

He felt two of my dreams were like that – the one when I dreamt my father's death the night before it happened, and the one when I dreamt I gave my father back his ring, and then it disappeared the next day. Zayde had an inkling there might be more to come with them. And as with a lot of things, it turned out he was right.

Some years later, one day, by coincidence, I ran into my old high school friend Marty in a grocery store. The morning after I dreamt that my father died, I had told him about it on our ride to school. I hadn't seen him in quite a while, and it just so happened that the day we met was Dec. 3, the anniversary of my father's death. After catching up with each other for about a half hour, I finally decided to ask him about the dream.

"Marty, I hope you don't mind if I ask you kind of a weird question," I started.

"You don't have to ask," he interrupted me. "You dreamt that your father died the night before it happened, and you told me about it the next day when we were driving to school. You dreamt that he died, it all came true, and I'll never forget it."

When I told Zayde about it, he just smiled and said, "See? You just got a confirmation and you don't have to doubt it anymore. It really did happen."

About six months later, one Saturday night, I was at a party and out of nowhere, a friend came over to me and said he had to tell me about an odd dream he had just had. In the dream, a stranger introduced himself. "I am David Richman's father," he said, "and I want you to give him a message for me." Then he showed my friend that he was wearing a ring. Suddenly, the ring started glowing with light and the man said, "Tell David I said—remember the ring." Then he repeated himself. "Give David Richman this message. Tell him I said to remember the ring."

When I told Zayde about it, he was transfixed. The fact that the dream had come to a complete stranger, an unbiased third party with no prior knowledge about any of it, was stunning. "And don't forget about the message," he said to me. "What did Dad want your friend to tell you?"

"He said I should remember the ring," I said.

"And what happened to the ring?" he asked.

"I don't know," I responded. "He told me to give it back to him. I did, and it turned into light. Then the next day, it disappeared out of my locked locker."

"And what does that tell you?" he asked.

I thought about it for a minute, but nothing really came to mind. "I don't know."

"Either do I," he said with a bemused smile. "And that's why it's such a great message. It gives you a lot to think about. The ring turned into light in the dream, then it disappeared the next day in real life. Maybe that means there's a connection between the two realms.

"And he told you a lot of things in that dream. He said there's no death. He said God wants you to think about him. Maybe he's telling you to remember the things he told you. Maybe you should give it more thought.

"Or maybe he told you to remember the ring because when you both held it, it connected you, like a bridge between you. Maybe he's telling you that the bridge is still there, that you're still connected, even beyond death.

"And you know what else? The ring turned into light and you felt yourself get pulled into it. What was that like?" he asked me.

"It was incredible," I said.

"Exactly," he went on. "Maybe, it even took you to Shamayim (heaven)? And maybe he's telling you to remember what that feeling was like, what that peace felt like? Maybe that was real.

"It's just like a lot of other things in life. Maybe none of it was real. Maybe some of it was real. Or maybe all of it was real. Who knows? I do know one thing, though—you have the rest of your life to figure it out."

His eyes were twinkling, and he gave me one of his warm, impish smiles. He did this kind of thing all the time, he'd use the word "maybe" in the tradition of the great Talmudic teachers he'd studied for years. They don't tell you things. They just plant seeds and help you let them grow.

***

As the months went by, every part of my life kept getting better and better. I was enjoying senior year of high school with my term as president, and my teenage love affair with Sally was in full bloom, quickly becoming the best thing that had ever happened to me. And the 76ers were absolutely on fire.

Wilt was still the same charismatic, larger-than-life figure as always, except for one thing. Now he was the undisputed king of the NBA, and the championship was finally within his grasp. By the end of the season, we posted a 68—13 record, which was unheard of at the time. And most of the victories were by more than 10 points.

When the playoffs came, finally this year, the contest with the Celtics was never in question. We blew them out in 5 games. In the clincher, which was at home, with a few minutes left, the crowd started chanting, "Boston is dead! Boston is dead!" They kept it going, over and over, stomping their feet in rhythm. In one way, there was something a little sickening about it, like being in the Roman Colosseum at a gladiator fight. But at the same time, it felt great because we were finally breaking a ten-year curse.

Anyway, we went on to play San Francisco for the

title. It was a surprisingly tough series, but in the sixth game, we finally wrapped it up out there. So, just three years after he formed them, and a year and a half after his historic trade for Wilt, my father's transplanted team, with the name he chose, the Philadelphia 76ers, were now the Champions of the World.

***

In 1967, Philly was one of those serious sports towns with a devoted fan base that hardly ever got to celebrate a championship. Including baseball, football, basketball, and hockey, this was only the fourth time in over sixty years that we had finished on top. The entire city was ecstatic.

The next day, when the team flew back to Philadelphia, my brother and I went to the airport and joined about five hundred fans to welcome home our heroes. We were standing with Vince Miller, Wilt's closest friend, and the rest of the team's front office, along with the players' wives and families. There were about fifty of us, gathered in a special area.

As we waited for the plane to land, I thought about my father and all the aggravation he had gone through that led to this point. In the beginning, the fans couldn't have cared less about the team and nobody came to the games. Now here we were, NBA champs, with the greatest record in league history and the whole city about to explode with pride. It was a shame he couldn't be there.

The plane finally landed. A few minutes later, the double glass doors opened, and the team came walking into the airport lobby to a huge cheer. Wilt was in the center, leading them. A constant stream of flashbulbs exploded from the press cameras, and he looked like a giant, walking through a lightning storm. I could see he was carrying a basketball in his hands.

As soon as he spotted my brother and me, he walked over to us, leaned down, and handed us the ball. "Give this to your mother for me," he shouted above the pandemonium. "And give her my love."

Later, I read that in the locker room after the championship game, the team had voted to give Wilt the game ball. He accepted but said that it really only belonged to one person – Clare Richman. He was going to give it to her. Nobody disagreed. He took careful custody of it and held it on his lap the whole flight home.

He stood there with us for another moment, then, he turned to walk away. But he turned back and grabbed me with his huge right hand, pulled me next to him, leaned down and whispered in my ear. "We did it, Davy. And we did it for him."

He patted me on the back, tousled my hair, and walked off into the adoring crowd.

40

He Knows Who He Is

The championship reign of the 76ers only lasted for that one season. In 1968 something changed. The magic was gone, and once again, the Celtics beat us in the playoffs. And then unexpectedly, Wilt demanded to be traded to the Lakers. Nobody knows exactly what happened, but he didn't want to play for Philly anymore. The trade was executed, and the City of the Angels welcomed him with opened arms.

He and I stayed in touch with each other. A few years later, I had a summer job with the San Francisco 49ers. When I took a break and went down to LA, Wilt invited me to visit him in his new home. I went out to see him one Saturday morning.

He had leveled off a cliff on the highest point overlooking Bel Air and had built an amazing modern mansion on it. The view was spectacular. From one side, you could see the whole city; from the other, you could see all the way to the ocean.

The house itself looked like a wild jazz improvisation, frozen in stone. There wasn't a single right angle in the place, and an indoor/outdoor swimming pool fed water into a stream that flowed through the living room. All the rooms were gigantic, with ultrahigh ceilings, and it was a real pleasure to see him in an environment that fit him. He wasn't stuck in a dollhouse anymore.

When he showed me around the grounds, I noticed that he had a great driveway for a basketball court, but he hadn't put one up. "No basket?" I asked.

"No. I don't want any of that here. This is where I relax." He looked over the vast panorama, toward the ocean. "I don't want anything to do with work here." As strange as it may seem, that was the first time it really hit me that basketball was Wilt's job. It was work to him. It might seem completely obvious, but to me, it was always a game, filled with glamor, money, and fame. But to him, it was his job. And from the look on his face, it was a hard job, too.

We went back inside, sat down in the den, and for some unfortunate reason, our conversation went straight to politics. The country was in a horrible state of turmoil over the war in Vietnam, and things kept getting worse. As it happened, Wilt and I were on opposite sides of the political fence.

I was in college, and like a lot of kids in my generation, I was going through some radical 60's changes. I wasn't a total hippie yet, but I was clearly heading in that direction, in both look and outlook. And to my extreme disappointment, as well as embarrassment, Wilt had endorsed Richard Nixon in the 1968 presidential election. It was big news, and the campaign really hyped it up.

The election year of 1968 had been an absolute disaster. Martin Luther King, Jr. and Bobby Kennedy were assassinated within two months of each other. King was killed exactly one year to the day after he announced his opposition to the war. And Kennedy, who was clearly opposed to it, was murdered the night he won the California primary, which had virtually assured him the Democratic nomination. So, two great American lights had been extinguished. On top of being incredibly depressing, it was downright scary.

And now Nixon, who had turned into a political ghost after 1960, had come back from the dead, and was running the war machine like a madman at the helm. But Wilt was really impressed with him, thought he had a brilliant mind, was a fiscal conservative, and a genius at foreign affairs. He had all the makings of a great president.

I couldn't have disagreed with him more. To me, Nixon was responsible for the deaths of hundreds of thousands of innocent people, the war was an atrocity, and he was making it worse. Supporting him was absolutely insupportable.

Even though we kept it polite, it kept getting more contentious, and the more we talked, the farther apart we got. Finally, the gulf between us was so big, we had nothing more to say to each other and just sat there in an awkward silence. I felt bad, but I didn't see any way out of it. We were stuck.

"Hey, I gotta good idea," Wilt said out of nowhere, flashing me one of his million-dollar smiles. "Why don't we go out for some pancakes? There's a great place I gotta show you in Beverly Hills."

The world of politics evaporated in an instant, and before I knew it, we were riding in this incredible sports car he had. It had been custom-built for him by some company I'd never heard of. He said it had the most powerful engine in the world, and once we hit the freeway, he really let it rip.

People used to criticize Wilt for his expensive taste in cars, but he knew what he was doing. He would drive them for a few years and then sell them while they still had relatively low mileage. Because it was "Wilt Chamberlain's old Bentley" or "Wilt Chamberlain's old Ferrari," they would sell at a high premium. He'd make a nice profit and have a great time doing it. Not a bad operation.

We cruised around with the top down in whatever this thing was and pulled up to the restaurant. As we walked in, I noticed he was carrying something the size of a brick, wrapped in white paper. When he plopped it down on the table, I could see the logo of the Sands Casino printed in gold on it.

We had a great time at breakfast. I think he ordered almost everything on the menu. He asked me if I was still together with Sally. He hadn't seen her in a few years, and I was really impressed he still remembered her name. Then, he asked about my mother, how she was doing and if she was seeing anyone. I gave him an update. She was coming along well and had taken a full-time job at an engineering firm in town. She had gone out with a few different men, but nothing had come of it. She was still flying solo.

After we finished our meal, the waitress brought us the check. Wilt pulled over the Sands package and opened it. I could see two stacks of one-hundred-dollar bills. Each stack had a large band wrapped around it with the number 100 printed on it. In about half a second, I did the math and figured out that he had twenty grand in hundreds sitting on the table in front of us. Even by today's standards, that's a lot of cash. Back then, it was astronomical.

He pulled out one of the hundreds and gave it to the waitress with the check. I didn't say anything, but I must have had a funny look on my face. "Oh, I was playing craps in Vegas the other night, and I didn't get a chance to go to the bank yet," he said as he re-wrapped the paper around the bills. It didn't close all the way, and you could still see some of the money.

At that point, he reached over and put his hand on my forearm. "David, I really do owe everything I have to your dad. I really do," he said and glanced down at the stack of hundreds. "You know how easy it would have been for me to blow all the money that was coming to me? It happens all the time. But your father kept me safe. Did you know he used to give me an allowance? I had to report everything I spent to him, like I was his kid. He was always lecturing me about asset appreciation, telling me to – plant your money where it will grow."

"And you know what?" he paused and polished off his cup of coffee. "Everything he put me in turned into gold. Every single deal. There are so many times when I think, 'God, if I could just talk to Ike about this.' And sometimes, I still go to pick up the phone and call him. Then, I remember that he's gone." He put his things together and got out his keys. "I know I'll never meet anyone like him again. He was really something else."

We got up, left the restaurant and started walking down the street to his car. He was casually carrying the wrapped-up money in his hand as we strolled along. Everybody we passed recognized him but quickly looked away. This was LA, not Philly. Celebrities were all over the place, and it wasn't cool to make a big deal out of seeing one.

"Don't you think it's a little crazy, walking down the street with all that money in your hands?" I asked him, once we got into the car.

"Why?" he asked, as if the question made no sense.

"Well, somebody might want to rob you," I answered, stating the obvious.

"Oh," he replied with a blasé tone. "Well, you know

what? They'd have to try to take it from me, first."

He ignited the magnificent sports car and gave the motor a few revs. It roared back at him, like a hungry lion, ready to devour the road. We cruised through some back streets, wending our way to the highway entrance, then took off.

The sun was out, and we flew through the wind. As I looked over at him with his dark shades and cool, relaxed smile, I thought of a line I'd read in a great newspaper profile about him: "One thing you can always say about Wilt Chamberlain—he knows who he is." It was true. The man had no doubt, and I loved that about him.

***

I didn't see Wilt again for a few years, when we met at a book-signing party in the spring of 1974. He had co-written a book called Wilt—Just Like Any Other 7-Foot Black Millionaire Who Lives Next Door.

It had just come out and was already a national phenomenon. The publisher was hosting a glamorous premiere party in Manhattan, and Wilt invited us to attend. My brother and Gotty were coming up by train, so my mother and I drove up together.

It was a gala event. When we walked into the reception room, it was filled with a few hundred people, and Wilt was standing down front, autographing books. We started walking down the center aisle toward him. At one point as we got closer, he looked up and saw us approaching. Suddenly, he got overcome with emotion. It rocked him back on his heels a little and his eyes filled up with tears. He turned away for a couple of seconds and quickly regained his composure. Then he looked back at me.

Nobody else had seen it, but we both knew what had happened. He had been surprised by the sight of my mother and almost started crying. It was our own private secret. And as we looked at each other, it reminded me of old times, when we lived in our own world.

He came over, kissed my mother, shook my hand, and went back to autographing books, laughing and making wisecracks, to everyone's delight. As I watched him, head and shoulders over everyone else, I realized that all my life, I'd seen some of the strongest men in the world try to push him around on the basketball court. They would lean against him, elbow him, and hit him with everything they had. And as powerful as they were, they could never budge him. Not even an inch.

But the sight of my mother, this petite, middle-aged woman, brought back fond memories of a time gone by, and of an old friend who was no more, and it nearly knocked him off his feet. Nothing moves the body or the mind like the heart.

41

The Ranger's End

A few months later, in December 1974, my father's father, Zayde, passed away. He was eighty-four, a ripe old age for the time. He had lived alone since my grandmother had died a few years earlier. He cooked his own food and was in great health—never hospitalized or even sick. And every day, he would walk the two miles to his Orthodox synagogue, where he would pray, do a few chores, and tutor some bar mitzvah boys.

We had always been close and of course, we got closer after my father died. But one day in 1972, unexpectedly it went to a deeper level. We were watching a NASA moonwalk on TV and he said it was a fake, and that they were really doing it in a TV studio.

When I asked him why he felt that way, he told me about a prayer they used to say monthly in the old country on the full moon. Apparently, this ancient prayer got dropped and never made it over here. Then he recited it—"The moon is so far away from the Earth. And in the same way, God's perfection is far away from man. But one day man will touch the moon, and when he does, know that the days of the Kingdom of Heaven on Earth have begun."

I had never heard that prayer before and even though it intrigued me, I didn't say anything. In truth, I had been keeping something from him and didn't want to discuss anything to do with God or religion.

During my recent college years, I had gotten a strong dose of the new hippie lifestyle, along with some of its mind-altering components. It was a wild time. As comedian Robin Williams once said, "If you can remember the Sixties, you weren't really there." Well I really was, and it really changed me.

I had gotten exposed to a lot of the New-Age thinking of the day, including different forms of eastern philosophy, personal growth and self-awareness. And I had started practicing a form of meditation which was having a profound effect on me as well. I was simply outgrowing a lot of my childhood concepts.

This kind of thing is pretty common in Judaism, and the hippy/spiritual movement of the Sixties had more than its fair share of Jewish kids. It makes sense, because the religion basically teaches you to think for yourself and not just accept things at face value. There's no hierarchy, no pope, or doctrine of infallibility. On the contrary, the spiritual leaders, the rabbis, are all just ordinary people, with plenty of ordinary faults. Your point of view is as valid as the next guy's.

In a way, it can be an un-religious religion, and it's been shaped into a million different forms. There are tons of non-observant Jews who don't practice the rituals, but revere the wisdom and love the culture, especially the food and the humor. And in their hearts, they are still very Jewish.

Regardless, I didn't want to talk to my grandfather about any of it. He was an old man and had been through enough "tsuris" in his life. (Yiddish for trouble). He didn't need any more. I was certain that my expanding point of view would only upset him, so I stayed away from it.

"So, you see," he said, pointing to the lunar surface on the TV screen, "This isn't real. It can't be. If they were really on the moon, the Kingdom of Heaven would be on its way."

"Actually, Zayde," I heard myself say, "it is real."

"What?" he asked, like he hadn't heard me right.

"Yes. It is real. All the prophecies are coming true and the whole planet is moving into a higher state. The Kingdom of Heaven IS at hand."

I couldn't believe those words had come out of my mouth. Even though I hadn't planned on saying anything to him, my tongue had been faster than my mind.

But the truth of the matter was, that's really the way I felt. I had spent four turbulent years in college in Washington DC, front and center at the demolition of the American status-quo. And my generation had been on the vanguard of a revolution that had transformed the world. For baby boomers, since Woodstock, the old order of "might-makes-right" was crumbling, and a new awareness was arising. The stirring messages of unity and peace were everywhere—in the music, the movies, on TV and the stage. It really did seem like the dawning of the Age of Aquarius, with mystic crystal revelation and the mind's true liberation, as they sang in the mega-hit musical "Hair." Millions of us believed it, and the high times were global.

Still, I hadn't meant to say anything to him. He came from another era, a distant time and place. He had been a Yeshiva student, and as a part-time cantor, was a full-time, orthodox Jew.

"What?" he shot back at me sharply, "What did you say?"

I thought he sounded angry and I scrambled around

in my mind to find a way out. But as I looked at him, I realized he wasn't angry; he was hungry. And alive with curiosity. From that moment on, and for the rest of his life, all we ever talked about was higher consciousness. He was like a sponge and wanted to know everything I knew. And the more I learned, the more he wanted to know.

He had no conflict with what I was doing either, which completely amazed me. He just wanted to gather as much knowledge about God and the higher realms that he could. He didn't care where it came from. I once asked him about it and he said, "Your religion's like a car. You drive it to get somewhere, and when you get there, you get out. It's the same thing with religion. It's supposed to get you to God. And when you do get to God, you leave everything else behind and go straight to him. Never forget that, Davy. Go straight to him."

***

As time went by, he was getting more and more otherworldly and I started visiting him every few days. He was always happy and cheerful, but the end was clearly in sight.

"Hi, Zayde," I said when I walked in on one of those last days. "What are you doing?" I was referring to the fact that he was walking toward the dining room.

"Oh, I'm just waiting now," he said. "That's all I'm really doing. Just waiting."

"What?" I asked.

"Just waiting. You know, I'm just waiting for him to take me." He raised his eyes up, toward the ceiling. "I really don't know why he hasn't yet. Most of my people are gone, and there's not much left for me to do here anymore. So, I'm just waiting for him to take me."

He sounded like a passenger sitting in a bus terminal, whose bus had been delayed. He didn't mind. He knew it was coming sooner or later. And he was happy to be finally going home.

He sat down and started eating his lunch. I glanced around the place. It was exactly the same as always—same family pictures on the wall, same furniture, down to the old black and white TV set. To him, they hadn't gotten color right yet, so he stayed with his original console.

I remembered sitting in front of it with him, watching The Lone Ranger, his Kal-El, vessel of God. At the end of each episode, Zayde would explain its deeper meaning to me, as the daring and resourceful Masked Rider of the Plains would give us a wave, and ride off into the sunset, ready to right the next wrong.

***

The last time I saw my grandfather, he was sitting at his dining-room table, about to eat lunch. He began every meal with a small glass of schnapps. He had one on his plate and downed it like water. He started eating, but soon, after just a few bites, he fell sound asleep. His head was resting on his chest, and I wasn't sure if he was still breathing. He had a faint smile on his face, like a baby, falling asleep to a lullaby.

At that moment, I could really see the family resemblance between him and my father. And as I looked at him, smiling in his sleep, I remembered my father's face, as he was lying in his coffin. He was smiling too. Of course, he was dead, but still, he looked like he was having a great time.

I had often thought about that smile and wondered— was the reason he looked so happy because he actually was?

Had he made the glorious transition into a higher reality, like the psychic said in that Lincoln letter? I wondered if there really was such a thing as a higher reality. And if there was, do you really have to die to get there? It didn't seem to make sense. Why can't you know that level of happiness now, while you're still alive?

My father had told me in my dream, that death was just a public relations stunt that God does to get people to think about him. If that's true, I really had to hand it to him. The whole thing certainly had me thinking.

After another minute, Zayde started to move a little. He lifted his head off his chest, opened his eyes and his slight grin turned into a happy smile. "Well, it won't be long now," he said cheerfully. Obviously, he was referring to the fact that he was about to die. But if anything, he was glad. He went on with his lunch, but when he finished, he looked at me somewhat seriously.

"Listen to me, Davy, and pay attention now," he said. "We came to this Earth to learn. And not just about anything. We came here to learn about the highest. And I'm going to tell you something important. When we leave here, we do get to keep what we learned. In fact, that's the only thing we get to keep. All the rest just goes back to dust."

He got up and started walking me toward the front door. I figured he was going to take a nap when I left. "So, learn what you came here for, and don't get too distracted by all the other stuff. You know what I mean? Most of what's here isn't really real."

We got to the door and he turned and looked at me. "In the morning, always say to yourself—I want to accomplish what I really came here for. And then, at the end of every night ask yourself—what did I learn today that brought me closer to God? Remember, it isn't what happens here that matters. It's what you learn. That's what it's all about." With his soft, contented smile in the afternoon sunlight, he really looked like the embodiment of a learned soul.

"The higher your understanding gets, the more gratitude you feel in your heart," he said. "And when you leave here with a heart filled with gratitude, you've done your job. Then the journey was worth the trip."

He put his right hand on the crown of my head and said some prayer in Hebrew that I didn't recognize. His pale-blue eyes were lit by a warm, steady flame, and he gave me a soft stroke on the cheek. "So long, Tot-a-la," he said. We hugged each other, and I left.

A few days later, as he was giving a bar mitzvah lesson in the synagogue, he died peacefully among the ancient texts.

42

Epilogue: Back to The Garden

In May 2007, Ike Richman and Irv Kosloff were inducted into the Philadelphia Sports Writers Hall of Fame as the founders of the 76ers. A ceremony was held, followed by a formal dinner. Our families were invited to speak at the induction and Koz's son, Ted, asked me to talk on behalf of both our families. He and I sat together on the podium, and his mother, Libby, was in the audience. Our parents, Clare and Ike and Libby and Koz, had been the closest of friends. Now, she was the only one left.

Koz had died back in 1995 at the age of eighty-two. He and I had always been close, and our bond lasted until the end. He was a unique individual, a purely self-made man, with a level of depth that very few people knew.

Libby, who was ninety-three at the time, was still living alone in the same home they had bought back in the fifties. She was still driving and going out to lunch with her family and friends. And she was still every bit as sweet as ever.

My mother had passed away almost twenty-five years earlier from Alzheimer's disease. It got her at an early age, and she fought it with everything she had. But inevitably, it took her apart, piece by piece. Besides being a wonderful mother, she was also one of the bravest people I've ever known, and I still miss her every day.

At the ceremony, they started showing some old clips of Wilt and the 76ers. As I watched, I drifted off, into my own memories of the days gone by. I could see Wilt, sitting in my father's office, the two of them conferring in their own private world, hatching their future plans. I pictured him signing those papers behind the curtain at the playoff game, my father pointing to lines on the contracts and Wilt signing them, barely looking down. Then following him into the arena, as the crowd went nuts at the sight of him.

I remembered our car rides, the miniature golf game at the shore, and all those nights stretched out on the floor, playing cards. Then I pictured the four of us, my mother, Wilt, Ike, and me, sitting around the kitchen table having dinner, talking and laughing. Even though it had been over forty years, the fond memories were still alive, and still beautiful.

"And now, please welcome Ike Richman's son, David," I heard the emcee say, bringing me back to the present. I started my talk by describing the lifelong friendship between my father and Koz. Then I went into the early days of the team and the trade for Wilt. And of course, I told some anecdotes.

After the ceremony, there was a short reception and I must have shaken hands with fifty people. Almost everyone had a story about Wilt. One stayed at the hotel in the Catskills when he was a bellhop there. Another was in Hershey the night he scored a hundred points and ran on the court and shook his hand. One saw him at a frozen custard stand in Overbrook and they had cones together. And on and on.

The Big Dipper (his favorite nickname) had passed away from heart disease about eight years earlier. For me, among many other things, he was my hero, my part-time roommate and the coolest guy I had ever known. He was also my father's tallest son.

***

As dinner ended, someone about my age introduced himself to me. He was from Cheltenham and his younger brother had been in my wife's class, but we had never met before. "David, there's something that I've always wanted to tell you, but I never got the chance," he said. "I was in the Boston Garden the night your father died."

Now that was a real shock. In all these years, I had never spoken to anyone who was there, outside of the team. "Wow," was all that came out of my mouth.

"I was going to BU (Boston University) at the time, and I had tickets to the game." He stopped, as if waiting to see if I wanted to hear about it. Maybe he thought it would be too painful for me, but the exact opposite was true. I was all ears.

"Wow," I said again, dumbfounded. "What happened?"

"Well, first of all," he began, "it was unbelievably intense in The Garden that night. The crowd was completely insane. And there's something vicious about those Boston fans. They can get really ugly up there. They have a mean streak in them, and it was out in full force. And let me tell you something, they hated Wilt. I mean they absolutely hated him. The second they saw him, they were screaming bloody murder at him, and they wouldn't let up. It was brutal and there was a really bad feeling in the air. To tell you the truth, it was kind of sickening."

For me, suddenly hearing this was about as unexpected as getting hit by lightning on a sunny day. Up until then, it had been a warm celebration of nostalgic old times. Suddenly, I was transported back to the Boston Garden, the night my father died.

"The pace of the game was furious, like the championship was on the line, and the fans were going crazy on every play," he continued. "I remember it was pretty early in the first period when your dad collapsed at courtside. Everything stopped until the medics came and carried him out. It was really horrible. My mind goes kind of blank here, because the next thing I can remember, the teams were coming out for the second half."

He paused and took a drink of water. The game had been forty-three years ago, but looking at him, it could have been last night.

"When they came back out onto the floor, I'll never forget it. Wilt looked like he was ready to kill somebody. The expression on his face was as hard as stone, but he was on fire. As soon as the half started, everybody knew to stay the hell out of his way. He was on a whole other level and they couldn't touch him. He was all over the place, blocking shots, grabbing rebounds and dunking the ball. But it wasn't just that, he was doing it all with a vengeance. All the other guys were right there with him, every one of them. Except for Dolph Schayes. Dolph was just dead. I don't think he even watched the game."

Now, of course, I had read all this in the papers a hundred times, but that was just journalism. This was a face-to-face, blow-by-blow, passionate account, from someone who was there and really cared. And I was getting it full blast. The scene had come alive in my mind like never before, and something within me wanted to drink in every part of it.

"The most incredible thing, David, was that The

Garden went dead silent. For the rest of the game, it sounded like they were playing in an empty parking garage. You could have heard a pin drop.

"And there was something about that hollow, echoing sound that really got me. The place had been filled with so much hate for us and Wilt. And now, everybody felt like he had personally shut them up. I was so proud of him.

"He had the ball when the final horn blew. He just slammed it down hard on the court and stormed off to the locker room. Everyone was stunned and for a little while, nobody moved."

That was the end of it. Neither of us spoke for a moment. There was nothing to say. He had finally gotten to tell me his story, and I had finally gotten to hear it. We were both touched, and I thanked him from the bottom of my heart.

***

A couple of months later, toward the end of the summer, our whole family was together at a large wedding.

My sister, Sybil, had become a gifted Special-Ed teacher. For over fifty years, our "wild Indian," had been teaching children with severe mental handicaps in the Philadelphia school system, enriching the lives of thousands of the city's neediest kids and their families.

My brother, Mike, has enjoyed a distinguished career as an attorney and served as Cheltenham Township's judge for over twenty years. A well-loved pillar of the community, he was also the longtime president of its volunteer fire department. In his office, he still has a sign that reads: "A truly rich man is one who is happy with what he has."

And me? I've had a pretty lucky run. I've been a writer and speaker in the field of personal growth, and most importantly, a practitioner as well. In a lot of ways, it's been an unconventional path and while I do have my fair share of scars, the view has certainly been well-worth the climb.

At the wedding reception, I was standing by myself for a few minutes, next to a large picture window. It was a bright, sunny afternoon in August, and some beautiful white swans were gliding on the surface of the lake below.

My brother walked over to me, along with a friend named Sonny Hill. Mike had just gotten back from Europe. And Sonny, a Philadelphia legend in his own right, had been a member of Wilt's inner circle. They wanted to hear about the Hall of Fame dinner.

I gave them a quick overview and then told them how I'd unexpectedly heard about the night my father died in The Garden. I went into all the details of my friend's story of Wilt's performance, and how he dominated the game, completely silencing the crowd. They were both deeply moved. After I finished, Sonny looked at me for a moment, with a noble expression on his face.

"You know what Wilt was doing, don't you?" he asked me. "He was paying tribute to your father." It was one of the most profound remarks I'd ever heard, summing up a thousand truths in one short sentence.

A waiter came by and gave us each a glass of champagne. We stood there for a moment, and then, as if the instinct hit us as at the same time, we raised our glasses in our own tribute. "To Wilt and Ike," Sonny said. We clinked our glasses together and drank a toast in their honor.

I finished the champagne and looked out at the lake. Two magnificent swans floated across the still water and disappeared into the golden sunlight.

The End

Appendix One

Wilt's NBA Records that Still Stand

Wilt Chamberlain holds 71 NBA records, 62 by himself.

By the Game

Most points in a game
100 by Wilt Chamberlain,
Philadelphia Warriors (vs. New York Knicks) on March 2, 1962

Most points in a half
59 by Wilt Chamberlain,
Philadelphia Warriors (vs. New York Knicks) on March 2, 1962 (2nd)

Most field goals made in a game
36 by Wilt Chamberlain,
Philadelphia Warriors (vs. New York Knicks) on March 2, 1962

Most field goals attempted in a game
63 by Wilt Chamberlain,
Philadelphia Warriors (vs. New York Knicks) on March 2, 1962

Most field goals made in a half
22 by Wilt Chamberlain,
Philadelphia Warriors (vs. New York Knicks) on March 2, 1962 (2nd)

Most field goals attempted in a half
37 by Wilt Chamberlain,
Philadelphia Warriors (vs. New York Knicks) on March 2, 1962 (2nd)

Most field goals attempted in a quarter
21 by Wilt Chamberlain,
Philadelphia Warriors (vs. New York Knicks) on March 2, 1962 (4th)

Most field goals made in a game, no misses
18 by Wilt Chamberlain,
Philadelphia 76ers (vs. Baltimore Bullets) on February 24, 1967

Most free throws made in a game
28 by Wilt Chamberlain, Philadelphia Warriors (vs. New York Knicks) on March 2, 1962 (28/32) and 28 by Adrian Dantley, Utah Jazz (vs. Houston Rockets) on January 4, 1984 (28/29)

Most rebounds in a game
55 by Wilt Chamberlain,
Philadelphia Warriors (vs. Boston Celtics) on November 24, 1960

By the Season

Most minutes per game average
48.52 by Wilt Chamberlain, 1961–62

Most minutes
3,882 by Wilt Chamberlain, 1961–62

Highest points per game average
50.36 by Wilt Chamberlain, 1961–62

Most points
4,029 by Wilt Chamberlain, 1961–62

Most 50-point games
45 by Wilt Chamberlain, 1961–62

Most 40-point games
63 by Wilt Chamberlain, 1961–62

Most field goals made
1,597 by Wilt Chamberlain, 1961–62

Most field goals attempted
3,159 by Wilt Chamberlain, 1961–62

Most field goals missed
1,562 by Wilt Chamberlain, 1961–62

Highest field goal percentage
72.7% by Wilt Chamberlain, 1972–73

Most free throws attempted
1,363 by Wilt Chamberlain, 1961–62

Highest rebounds per game average
27.2 by Wilt Chamberlain, 1960–61

Most rebounds
2,149 by Wilt Chamberlain, 1960–61

Most consecutive triple-doubles
9 by Wilt Chamberlain, 1967–68

By Career

Most minutes per game
45.8 seconds, average by Wilt Chamberlain

Most consecutive seasons leading league in points
7 by Wilt Chamberlain (1959–60–1965–66) and
Michael Jordan (1986–87–1992–93)

Most 60+ point games
32 by Wilt Chamberlain

Most 50+ point games
118 by Wilt Chamberlain

Most 40+ point games
271 by Wilt Chamberlain

Most consecutive 50+ point games
7 by Wilt Chamberlain from December 16–29, 1961

Most consecutive 40+ point games
14 by Wilt Chamberlain from December 8–30, 1961
and January 11 – February 1, 1962

Most consecutive 30+ point games
64 by Wilt Chamberlain from November 4, 1961 – February 22, 1962

Most consecutive 20+ point games
126 by Wilt Chamberlain from October 19, 1961 – January 19, 1963

Most consecutive seasons leading league in field goals made
7 by Wilt Chamberlain (1960–66) and Michael Jordan (1987–93)

Most consecutive seasons leading league in field goals attempted
7 by Wilt Chamberlain (1960–66)

Most consecutive field goals made
35 by Wilt Chamberlain from February 17–28, 1967

Most seasons leading league in free throws attempted
8 by Wilt Chamberlain

Most rebounds
23,924 by Wilt Chamberlain

Highest rebounds per game average
22.9 by Wilt Chamberlain

Appendix Two

Wiltisms

In 1991, Wilt wrote a book of personal observations called "A View From Above." He wrote it entirely himself, without the use of a co-author. He was a much deeper thinker than most people knew and throughout the book, he interspersed short sayings that he termed, "Wiltisms." The following are some excerpts.

"Some say the last true winner is death. But does anybody know for sure? Could we just move on to play another game on another plane?"

"Wisdom is a strange commodity. The more you have, the more you realize how dumb you are."

"Enthusiasm can't be taught but can be caught."

"Size has never been a barometer for measuring the worth of a man. Unless you are talking about the size of his heart."

"Even a wise man seems like a fool among fools."

"Greed, envy, and fear are the cause of much human behavior. Too much."

"Compassion, goodwill, common sense, understanding, and love are just a few of the things in life that are free. Use them."

"It is said that good things come to those who wait. I believe that good things come to those who work."

"Of all our faculties, the most important one is our ability to imagine. Can you imagine how it would be not to be able to imagine?"

"The problem with doing nothing is that you never know when you are through. That's why it's so easy to keep on doing nothing."

"Everything is habit-forming, so make sure what you do is what you want to be doing."

"The one thing we know that we can control is
how much time we have before we grow old."

"We have become a society of hero worshipers. And
oh boy, what heroes! We have made some of the most
blasé, most average, most ridiculous people in the
world our heroes. Because a guy can dunk a basketball,
because a guy can hit a home run, all of a sudden he
becomes our hero. Do we have such little belief in
ourselves, are we so bored, that we create these tin
Gods so we have someone to follow? Aren't there
enough worthwhile things we can get our kids and
ourselves involved in and be proud of? I sure hope so."

"Can you imagine how much better life would be, by
allowing our minds and our thinking to be free?"

"We spend too much time feeding our bodies and not our
souls.
We spend too much time with what we wear
and too little time with how much we care."

"Ike Richman, the owner of the 76ers, sent me to a shrink
to see if that could help solve my problem. It didn't.
Ike was paying a hundred dollars an hour for me to
tell that psychiatrist my problems, which I did for four
months. All that happened is that the shrink became a
really good foul shooter and I became a good analyst."

Appendix Three:

Excerpts from Memorial Session of Philadelphia Court of Common Pleas, December 7, 1965

On the Tuesday following the funeral of Isaac Richman, a special session was held to allow his colleagues to officially speak on the record, eulogizing their fallen friend. The session was presided over by Hon. D. Donald Jamieson, President Judge, former partner and longtime friend. The following are some short excerpts from the lengthy procedure.

Marvin Comisky, Chancellor of the Philadelphia Bar Association

This is indeed a sad occasion. We, the Philadelphia Bar Association appreciate the convening of a special session of Court.

While Isaac Richman had other interests, aside from his family, the law had his prime affection. He was proud of being a lawyer. He was extremely devoted to his clients and always undertook a matter with a battlefield plan of action.

Many a legal opponent did not realize until too late, that Isaac Richman's jocular attitude and his apparent indifference to clauses in a proposed agreement, and his expressed desire to make a settlement, was all part of a master plan. He was smart. He was resolute. And he was resourceful...

On behalf of the lawyers practicing in the City of Philadelphia and as Chancellor of the Philadelphia Bar Association, I acknowledge our extreme regard for our deceased brother—an honest and worthy man.

Daniel Greenstein, colleague and partner

Ike Richman was a faithful and loyal friend and an untiring worker in the vineyard of worthwhile causes. He was a keen student of strong conviction and integrity, an ardent advocate and a gracious opponent.

He was an outgoing, bright, gregarious being, full of compassion, love and great humor, a delightful companion. He was everybody's contemporary, notwithstanding age, race or religion.

He devoted himself unceasingly to the needs of his fellow men in his own calling and in a legion of civic and religious organizations. Above all, Ike Richman was a devoted and loving son, husband and father. He has made a lasting imprint on the sands of time. I and many others will always remember him as an exemplary human being.

Isadore Shrager, colleague

If Ike gave his word, it was more binding and meaningful than the most meticulous, written document... Honesty, loyalty and fairness were the doctrines by which he practiced his profession and from these principles he never veered. Ike was a great negotiator because he always brought with him to the negotiating table a keen sense of fairness and straight-forwardness. He was always willing to give the other side the benefit of the doubt.

This past Sunday was black Sunday for thousands of his friends who, together with his immediate family and relatives paid their last respects. People from all walks of life sadly, silently and with dignity gathered at his funeral. Athletes, giants in size, cried like children. Young and old alike could not restrain their emotions. Sadness reigned.

James L Price, partner of twenty-five years

I would like to address myself this morning to the inner personality and philosophy of this man whom we have gathered here today to memorialize and honor...

From what I have called the top of his desk, under the glass top was a collection of writings gleaned from many sources that through the years had appealed to him, because they had expressed clearly his own sentiments on the subjects which were recorded. It is of these that I would tell you so that a record might be made—

A quote from Lincoln—

"I do the very best I know how, the very best I can, and I mean to keep doing so until the end; if the end brings me out all right, what is said against me won't amount to anything.'

A quote from Douglass MacArthur—

"Build me a son, O Lord, who will be strong enough to know when he is weak, and brave enough to face himself when he is afraid; one who will be proud and unbending in honest defeat, and humble and gentle in victory.

Build me a son whose wish will not take the place of deeds; a son who will know Thee and that to know himself is the foundation stone of knowledge.

Lead him, I pray, not in the path of ease and comfort, but under the stress and spur of difficulties and challenge. Here let him learn to stand up in the storm. Here let him learn compassion for those who fail.

Build me a son whose heart will be clear, whose goal will be high, a son who will master himself before he seeks to master other men, one who will reach into the future, yet never forget the past.

And after all these things are his, add, I pray, enough of a sense of humor, so that he may always be serious, yet never take himself too seriously. Give him humility, so that he may always remember the simplicity of true greatness, the open mind of true wisdom and the meekness of true strength.

Then I, his father, will dare to whisper—I have not lived in vain."

Hon. D. Donald Jamieson, former partner and protegee

As most of you here know, Isaac Richman was probably my closest friend and critic. His passing is so recent and shockingly sudden that I feel his presence, looking over my shoulder as he did so many times while he was with us....

He was to me not merely a friend. More precisely, I was a member of his family and he, of mine....

And to you, Isaac Richman, for instilling in me something of your tremendous devotion to cause and client, I am indeed grateful. For teaching me directly and indirectly the high art of negotiation, of compromise and settlement, I am eternally grateful.

As has been mentioned here, negotiation was his professional strength. I have never seen, and while I am in this mortal coil, do not expect to see, Ike's equal or peer in this key phase of the law.

He was indeed the maestro and all others negotiating with him, willingly or not, were mere players who followed his composition. I thank him for the opportunity to see mutual love, affection, teamwork and respect in family life...

I am indeed a better man for having known him. There are a few people in my life to whom I owe more than I could ever repay. Isaac Richman was one.

And so we say to you, good-bye, Isaac Richman, we will miss you—'til we meet again.

The Better Angels Publishing Company

The mystic chords of memory...will yet swell... when again touched, as surely they will be, by the better angels of our nature.

— A. Lincoln

Our goal is to produce works that inspire and enlighten, as well as entertain. According to the wisdom of the ages, as well as modern science, all the noble virtues of human nature are within each one of us, simply awaiting our own self-discovery. Abraham Lincoln called them "the better angels of our nature." We seek to nurture these better angels, and as much as possible, to keep things light.

About David Richman

David Richman, President and Creative Director, has been a writer, researcher and speaker in the field of personal growth for over forty-five years. He is also a veteran advertising consultant, with an expertise in brand messaging. Combining his experience in both areas, his work seeks to present universal insights in simple ways that are enjoyable and easy to understand.

David is a graduate of American University. Since 1971, the foundation of his inner growth is based on the methods taught by internationally acclaimed teacher Prem Rawat. Additionally, along with decades of research, he is a certified trainer of Project Renaissance's Creative Problem-Solving Methods, has completed training in Positive Psychology: Dr. Martin Seligman's Visionary Science from the University of Pennsylvania, as well as Dr. Jean Houston's program on Quantum Mindfulness.

Photo by Jim Vuko

www.BetterAngelsPublishing.com